DEDICATATED TO

MATTHEW TO WHOM I AM SO PROUD

1

England in December 1938-specifically, the town of Lincoln. Outside, the still quiet evening sky turned to a cold dark snowy night. The ornate table light flickered, casting long dark shadows over the mountain of paper work that covered the oak desk of Detective Sergeant Ray Munroe. Ray looked towards the ornate table light; he gave the table a bang a few seconds later the table light flickered once more before sending the life of the office into darkness. Opening his lower draw of his desk, Ray rummaging through the mountain of files finally found what he was looking for, a spare bulb. He reached into his trouser pocket trying to locate his hankie. Just then, the phone started to rang; Ray taking a few moments placed the bulb down before he picked up the receiver. “Munroe”- he answered, silence “Munroe” he answered again, he was about to replace the phone back on to the cradle when the caller started to speak. Munroe, without speaking listened, the caller hung up after 5 minutes. After placing the receiver down, letting his hand rest on the phone for a while, thinking what the caller had said. He reached for his note pad and then started to jot down what the caller had said. After Munroe had finished writing, he tore the paper away from the notebook and placed the paper inside his jacket, patting once to make sure it was there.

Munroe checked the time 6.30pm. It was Christmas Eve 1938; another hour should sort out the paper work then it was time to head for home. At 8.45pm Munroe final placed his pen into his shirt pocket, slipped on his jacket making sure that the note was still inside then headed down stairs, stopping on the way to gaze outside the window, watching the snow falling. The duty sergeant on the desk was booking in a local drunk when DS Ray Munroe passed him, with a slight gesture of the arm to acknowledge that he had seen Him. Munroe grab the heavy wooden door handle to be-greeted by the bitter cold wind, snow was still falling. Munroe shifted his collar of his jacket around his neck to shield some of the bitter wind then headed down the steps towards his car. The car covered with at least 2 inches of snow, and still it was falling. Finally, after a few moments scraping snow away, Munroe managed to open the car door and switch on the engine. The roar of the Ford 10 brought to life the snow, which covered the scenery of Lincoln. Ray adjusted the heater control for maximum heat, selected reverse and gently manoeuvred the Ford out of the station. Munroe turned left onto Monks Road; snow covered both sides of the road making driving difficult. The tyres crunching the falling snow as he slowly drove towards Milman Road. Reaching the bottom of the hill Munroe stopped the Ford looked up towards the County Hospital and said aloud "the old girl won't make it". Selecting first gear Munroe eased the Ford slowly forward trying to gain a footing in the already snow covered road. The Ford 10 did not let him down, before long he was driving down Greetwell Road heading for East Gate another 20 minutes should see him home. Munroe drove on to the cobble stones of Bailgate; he stopped and looked at the mastic sight of the cathedral with its twin towers reaching sky wards like guarding angel's trying to catch the falling snow before it came, tumbling down. Turning left down Drwry Lane for a few snow-covered seconds Munroe noticed the street called Gibraltar Hill he was home.

Parking the old Ford 10 in the snow covered drive, Munroe noticed that the bathroom light on. Opening his car door

Munroe was soon, greeted by the far distance sound of a barking dog. The echo sounded like it was miles away, until he realised that it was his faithful companion Duke. Duke a Golden Retriever was found abandon almost two years ago as a very young puppy. Tide up and drenched to the bone, and almost starved to death Munroe took him home. Since their encounter both Ray and Duke have been inseparable. Closing the car door Munroe kneeled down as he had done for the past two years waiting until Duke bounded up. Duke stopped short sat down and waited until he was, given the command. Duke slowly walked up towards Ray, placing his front paws on both shoulders, they embraced for a short while before, Duke bounded back towards the house he called home. Closing the yard door behind him, Ray walked the few snow-covered steps until he reached the rear door which lead into the kitchen. The warmth hit him full in the face, hanging his jacket on the peg Ray watched as Duke laid down in his basket, curled up in a tight ball he was safe in the knowledge that his master was home. Ray Munroe made his way up stairs towards the bathroom, opening the door he found his wife Karen stretched out in the bath. The bubble bath positioned carefully to hide her nakedness; Ray's imagination was racing ahead of him knowing that his wife had the body of a model under all those bubbles. Karen opened her eyes when she heard the bathroom door opening, turning her head she looked and smiled at Ray, "had a good day" she said, "not bad are we still going to the White Hart" asking Ray. Karen lifted her hand full of water from the depth of the bath and threw the hand full of water towards Ray. The water hit him square in the face, laughing and wiping away the running water Ray edged closer to the bath and then placed his hand deep amongst the bubbles making his way towards Karen's midriff, instantly Karen placed her hand on his to stop him going any further. They both looked into each other's eyes the chemistry between them was second to none each full filling each other is pleasure when it came to the bedroom. Ray withdrew his hand and handed Karen a towel, watching as she slowly eased herself out of the tub. His eyes looking her up and down. Placing her hand across her breast, to hide her modesty calmly said "seen plenty then" Ray lifted his eyes to meet hers smiled then turned and walked to the bedroom to be changed.

Karen being a well to do lawyer worked for a leading team based in Lincoln. She first met Ray at a local police officer ball three years go. It was love at first sight for both of them. Ray was standing in a corner when Karen walked in; Ray a tall dark handsome person clean-shaven well educated had been with the police force for seven years and had gained the respect of his follow officers. He passed his exam for detective two months before he met Karen. Not long after that first meeting they had been, married Ray promoted to the rank of Detective Sergeant. Both shared the love of the outdoor way of life. Weekends after work they drove to the Lake District climbing and hill walking learning how to survive in the extreme weather condition, friends called them the action couple.

Ray's parents lived on the out skirts of Lincoln in a small hamlet of Ryland. His father like most fathers had fought in the First World War. He saw action with the Lincolnshire Regiment fighting in the Somme and later transferred to the new Tank regiment until the end of the war. His father highly decorated during those long and frightful years, and had retired with the rank of Brigadier in 1922.

Karen was born in France her Mother being of French origin and her Father English. Karan's father a highly positioned banker established himself at the Paris branch. With this soled combination of languages, Karen could speak fluent French with ease. When she had finished her education both her parents decided, it was time they should move back to London. Shortly after there, return Karen's father had to retire due to ill health. Karen moved to Lincoln when she passed her bars degree. Years passed her by with more court cases than she could handle. Her reparation followed her from county to county. Karen was happy in her job as well as going out to the nightclubs in Lincoln. One day, tragedy struck with the news that her parents had been, killed in a road traffic accident this unpleasant news almost finished Karen off until she met Ray Munroe. Close friend to Karen mentioned the police officer ball and had brought her along; Karen had a lot to thank her friend since that first meeting with Ray Munroe.

Munroe was standing in front of the mirror when Karen walked in trying to tie his bow tie, her nakedness gleaming in the twilight of the room with the only the table light casting long and cascading shadow's across her body. Ray watching thru the mirror, noticed her movement towards her chest of draws, she removed a slender PR of white underwear before slipping them on making sure that her bottom was the last part to be, covered followed by the suspender belt, it was if she was playing a game with Ray. Karen knew that Ray was watching her getting dressed; it pleased her that he still found her sexy and attractive. Ray turned round and said "you look beautiful", "well thankyou kind sir" said Karen. She came over and gave Ray a long and passionate kiss. Munroe Checked his watch it was time to go. Ray followed Karan down stairs into the kitchen; Duke was sitting in his basket waiting. Munroe helped Karen on with her coat looked at Duke and said "coming" with a wag of his tail, he made his way to the door waiting for his master to open it.

Once outside with the snow still falling they both headed off towards the White Hart. Duke ran a head trying to catch the falling snowflakes as he went. It was not long before they had reached the White Hart; outside they could both hear the piano playing Christmas tunes. Munroe parents were waiting near the open fire, Ray's father noticing their arrival beckoned them over. Karen walking a head kissed them both on the cheek, in a way that she had always done since she first met them. It was the way the French greeted people afterwards she turned and placed her arm through Rays. Duke had found his place near the fire to settle down for the evening. The property owner Harold Placeman had known both Ray and Karen for a long time. Ray first brought Duke into the bar when he was a pup, Harold looked at him smiled and said "you can come into my bar any time you like, the spot near the fire will all ways be yours" patting Duke gently on the head. Duke turned his head to one side and gave one of those looks that only dogs can give. Since that first encounter, Duke had always laid beside the fire the locals became friends he was one of the regulars.

Munroe's father taking his son by the arm led him to one side. His face looked like he had the world on his shoulders, "seen the head line in the local paper" (Ray looked into the face of his father; he knew that the headline might mean that WAR was looming over the cannel with this Hitler being in charge of Germany.) "I have sir" "will you be signing up" Munroe turned his head slightly to look at Karen then back towards his father. Then said, "I haven't given it much thought, as what I shall do". Ray knew in his heart his father wanted to see his son in the Army, like father like son he thought, but it would not be like the last war fighting in the trenches this war would be about weapons that no man had seen before, with more millions of people dying for no cause.

The last war was a war to end all wars so the paper had said back in 1918. Karen walked over to see what they were talking about; both Ray and his father looked at her strolling towards them. His father wisped in Ray's ear "you've got a cracker their son" Ray could not help but smile in the thought of what he had seen and witnessed in the bedroom. Munroe gave Karan a tender kiss on the cheek, then whispered "I love you". The evening carried on long after the old bells of the Cathedral had sounded midnight the beginning of Christmas Day 1938.

2

Christmas Day came with more snowfall during the night than was normal. Ray quietly eased himself to the edge of the bed trying not to wake Karen and walked over to the curtains, silently pulling them open. Looking through the window Ray noticed the snow covered rooftops the rising of the smoke from the tall brick chummy sending column's skywards. Ray's eyes darted from the scenery that was breathe taking the snow had just stopped falling from the night before the sun was trying to break through the morning sky it looked like it was going to be a good day. Ray heard the sound of the bed covers rustling, turning around he saw that Karen had thrown the covers of her naked body exposing herself to the delight of Munroe, her left hand resting between her thighs covering her pubic hair. Walking back to the bed Munroe moved closer to Karan placing his hands around her waist, Karan moaned then slowly opened her eyes looked at Ray and moved one of his arms to caress her right breast before kissing him full on the mouth. There love making lasted until they heard the sound of Duke barking down stairs. They both started to laugh aloud before Munroe got out from the bed grab his dressing gown and descended the stairs to the kitchen. Duke was waiting near the back door; unlocking it, Duke darted threw it on to the garden. He danced around until he found the place that would do as the toilet, satisfied with his effort Duke looked up when Munroe whistled him back inside. Closing the door behind him Munroe looked at Duke and smiled then walked back up to find Karen. Entering the bedroom, he noticed that Karen had got up and was having a bath, not wanting to waste the water Ray slipped his gown off and joined Karen, the love making continued.

Munroe parents had invited them for dinner at the manor for midday. It would take them the best part of an hour drive due to the weather condition. At 11o'clock carrying the Christmas presents they finally left but not before they got the Ford 10 clear of snow. Passing the White Hart, they both noticed that Harold was out clearing the snow away from the main porch; with the press of the car, horn Ray and Karen raised their arms in unison to wave. Harold placing both hands on his broom looked up and gave them a salute, finally watching them turn the corner before he carried on with the snow clearing. Deep snow covered the road leading the way to the manor. Reaching the out skirts of Lincoln, they soon entered the long straight country road that would take them through scenery of hanging branches, lakes that had frozen over. Roaming sheep in fields' heads were down looking for a blade of grass to eat and the deer, the male ones looking proud with their antlers shining in the midday light, and finally coming into view sitting on a hill stood the grandeur of the Munroe Manor. The building dated back to the18th century, all the Munroe descendants had been born there including Ray Munroe. Karen told Ray to stop at the tall brick pillars so she could look at the marvel of the building before Ray eased the Ford outside the front steps that lead to the main door. Before they had chance to open the car door the faithful footman appeared, "Good morning master Ray and Madam Karen," said John. "Morning John-Father up" "yes sir his is in the drawing room" Ray and Karen walked through the grand wooden door, the sight always lit up Karen eyes when she witnessed the staircase and the long hall. John took the coats from Ray and Karen and monitored them to the drawing room. Duke had already found his way. Rays father stood up when they walked in, Karen as in the White Hart went over and kissed him on the cheek, the men shook hands. John entered after a few minute with a slight knock on the door. John Knight had served as his batman during the Great War and had remained with him when Ray's father had asked him if he would like to join his household. The brigadier asked John if the mistress was going to join them, John cleared his throat and said "Mistress Elisabeth would be down shortly" "thank you John"

Ray walked over to open the French door windows to let Duke out and then followed him out Side lighting up a cigarette Karen joined him a few moments later. They both looked up when they heard the sound of an aircraft over head, clasping their hands to shield the gleam from the sun the lonely Wellington Bomber flew right over them dipping its wings as it did so, Karen stared "where do you think it might be going" not bothering to look at Ray. "It's heading towards Waddington," said Ray in amazements of the wonders sight, which they had just witnessed. The brigadier informed them that Elisabeth had joined them; which broke the thoughts and stillness of the Munro's. Ray placed his cold hand on to the back of Karen's dress a cold shiver went through her. Both entered the drawing room. Elisabeth walked over towards Karen placing both hands on her shoulders; she gave her a tender hug followed by the welcome kiss on both cheeks, Merry Christmas darling. The grandfather clock standing proudly in the hall stuck one 'o' clock lunch was ready.

The tradition of the Manor house that after lunch on Christmas day the men folk would leave the women and entertain them self in a spot of rabbit shooting. Karen had always joined in with this. She was a crack shot with the shotgun putting the men to shame on more than one occasion. Karen's father had shown her the art of shooting from a very early age. In her teens, Karen had entered the local game shoot coming joint second with the most kills. After they had all changed ready for the shoot, Ray waited down in the lobby for the arrival of Karen. Looking stunning as always Karen walked down the long wilding stair case to wards Ray and his father, both men with mouths wide open looked up when they heard her coming down, amassing how one could look so good in just a sigma of an outfit. Karen paused on the forth step from the bottom Posing as a modal advertising the outfit she was wearing laughing all the time.

Duke still outside, warmed himself in the late afternoon sun looked up when he noticed a hare running across the covered lawn cascading mountains of snow from its rear feet as it bounded through the deep packed snow. The hare soon made the safety of the far distance hedgerow, stopping and standing on its rear legs taking in the surrounding scenery before he finally turned away. Duke heard the sound of footsteps, looked at the ground the hare had covered, then turned his head waiting for the sound of his master voice.

Ray, Karen and the brigadier collected their cartridge belts along with the shotguns. The sun was still shining during the hours that the party was out for; feet covered in crust snow, they trudged back towards the warmth of the manor. Karen stated to thaw out in front of the fire, Duke by her side the rabbits been taken down to the cook. Ray with his father took a class of brandy in the study. They talked of what the imposed threat of war would mean to this country. His father asked again if Ray would be joining up. Ray placed his glass down and walked over to the log burning fire before turning round to look at his father, he was a proud man Ray knew. "Father my decision to join will depend on what Britain will do in the event of war" - in the meantime I'm still a policeman with a job to do" Ray's father with the bottle of brandy strolled over to Ray, topped up his glass then just smiled. The brigadier knew he would join up just give it time he thought.

Elizabeth along with Karen entered the study to find their husbands drinking what was left of the brandy bottle. "Any one for a game of bridge" said Elizabeth. Karen moved the table near to the fire. The men moved the chairs. "Who's partnering who then?" asked Karen. At the end, it was the men verse the women. The clock standing on the mantel peace above the warm fire chimed the hour of midnight with the last card hand being, dealt. "Good result" said Ray after they had won the last game. Karen looked at Elizabeth and whispered that they had cheated; both men laughed aloud got up and walked over to the drinks table. "Mines a G T," said Karen. Finally, it was time to call it a night; Karen made her way to the bedroom, after saying good night to Elizabeth and the brigadier while Ray let Duke out into the garden. Ray lit up a cigarette and watched Duke Bounce around the snow covered lawn. It had started to snow again. Ten minutes later Ray walked back inside. Duke laid down near the fire he would stay there until the morning, "good night old fella" said Ray, Duke lifted one ear before he finally closed his eyes.

Munroe entered the bedroom finding Karen naked lying face down, he moved closer caressing her toned bottom his hand working up towards her neck. Moaning with pleasure Karen turned over

Exposing her round and frim breast, Ray clasped each breast gently pinching the already erect nipples. Karen started to unbutton Rays clothing, his clothing thrown all over the bedroom floor. Munroe climbing over her legs lay down on top of her sucking each breast in turn; finally, Karen opened her legs to let Ray enter her. Ray slowly pushed himself inside slowly at first teasing her as he did so. Karen opened her self-wider wrapping her legs around his back to let Ray go deeper, thrusting harder each time before Karen finally climaxed with joy followed by Ray. Both stayed entwined for a while touching, kissing and caressing before Ray eased himself from her. Naked together they both held hands not bothering to talk; Karen turned on her side and wrapped her arms around Ray's chest before they both drifted off to a deep sleep.

The following morning found both Ray and Karen still entwined as they had been the night before. Munroe kissed her tenderly before he placed his feet on the carpet to draw the curtains open to let the morning light cascade itself through the bedroom. The sun was breaking through the cloud, the lonely icicle hanging from the guttering stood firm as if it was fighting with the element from the outside. Karen joined Ray at the window caressing his back moving her arms to hold him tight; Karen could sense the sexual turn on with Ray, she moved her hands lower towards his throbbing member. Munroe facing her noticed the pleasure in her eyes. He gently lifted her up; Karen wrapping her legs around his back exposing her self-wide so Ray could slide inside her, rocking up and down it wasn't long before they both came again, dipping with sweat Ray carried Karen to the bathroom, still locked together. Karen could still feel Ray's throbbing member deep inside her. She wanted him again and again, mentioning to Ray to sit down on the toilet seat Karen moved herself up and down taking her time getting the maxim pleasure, Ray feeling the pleasure of Karen started to caress her nipples, with the movement of Karen on top they soon became hard to the touch. It was not long before they both climaxed together, the best sex they had for a while. "We have to have the toilet seat again," laughed Karen.

Breakfast was in the dining room, Elisabeth and the brigadier where already down when they both opened the door. Munroe noticed that Duke was outside running around the lawn after a hare. Duke did not stand a chance in catching it but it was good exercise for him. John Knight entered the dining room with fresh bacon and eggs cooked by Elsa – May Woodcock the long-time cook who had been with the household for more years than Ray could remember. Ray Munroe announced that Karen and he would be returning back to Lincoln after breakfast, Ray was back on duty the following day, Elizabeth looked at Ray's father pleading with her eyes in finding a way that they could say longer. The brigadier new that his son had a job to do so nothing he said would change his mind, he just smiled and reached over to hold her hand in a movement and gesture of understanding. Breakfast over, Karen, excused herself and went back upstairs to pack the bags.

Duke was the first in the Ford 10; Karen gave them both a big hug and thanked the staff for all their hard work. Ray stepped forward to give his mother a kiss on both cheek's, his father stood proud as always shook his sons' hand. With the sounding of crunching snow beneath the tyres' Ray eased the Ford down the long drive passing the same landmarks as they had done the day before.

3

The journey back home through the snow-covered roads was uneventful apart from the sighting of a lonely hare dashing across the road in search of an undisturbed hedgerow. Entering the cobblestones of Bail Gate, turning left passed the White Hart the Munroe's noticed that Harold Placeman the property owner was outside again clearing the snow from the steps. He stopped for a breather heard the sound of a car and looked round to notice that it was his friends had just turned the corner. With hand on the broom, Harold waved them down. Karen wide her windows down to let the fresh cold air enter the Ford; shivers ran down her back making Karen clasp her hands around her slender shoulders. Harold leaning on his broom with one hand stepped forward to greet his friends. "Had a good Christmas then"? Karen looked across at Ray smiled, then turned towards Harold. "Yes thank you- you"? Harold said that they had been busy but managed to have a few hours to their selves before he opened up for the night session. Duke pushed his noise passed Karen shoulder when he realised that it was Harold, Harold patted his head. "In for a pint to night then" asked Harold. Ray said that they should be okay but it would not be for long. Easing his head from the car window Harold watched the Munroe's pull away, smiled then continued with the ever-endless task of snow clearing.

Duke dashed to the rear gate once he was out of the car, he was home. Ray collected the bags then followed Karen through the yard gate. Once inside the phone started to ring, picking up the receiver Ray looked at Karen and listened before placing the phone back on its cradle. "What's up?"

said Karan. Ray informed her that he had a case to attend too. "Can't it wait until tomorrow" asked Karan.
"Can't"
"Why not"
"It's a missing person, some sort of science person from London"
Ray whirled around crabbing the keys as he did so. Ray stopped short at the back door turned back looked at Karen blew a kiss then left.

Ray Munroe entered the police station to be, greeted by the duty sergeant. A telephone rang. The duty sergeant snapped up the middle one, which someone had marked as foremost with an urgent slash of showgirl's lip rouge." Yes, sir. DS Munroe.... Yes, sir! He is here... Yes, sir I will tell him. Good-bye sir.

The duty sergeant, cradling the phone. Turned then said to Ray Munroe, the DCI says if you do not get your backside in his office in five minute, you are, fired. DC John-Smith Patten was waiting on the stairs when Ray got to the top. "What up John" "Flap on, some big wig has gone missing" Munroe knocked on the door of DCI Carter.
"Come in"
"Sit down gentlemen"

DCI passed a file to Munroe, on top in red ink was the word "Secret" Looking over the file at Carter, then at John-Smith Patten, Munroe asked the underline question. "Why us" DCI Carter told them that he wanted the best and you are all I have. The call from the Met boys in London stated that this science person wife had phoned informing them that he was due home for Christmas but had failed to turn up, that was three days ago.
"Do we know what kind of work he did" asked Munroe. DCI Carter stood up and walked over to the window, gazed at the

sight of Lincoln with its snow-covered rooftops, after a short pause he turned around walked back to his desk, placed his hands on the file then uttered a sort sentence. Both Munroe and John – Smith Patten stared at each other, this science Professor person working for the government was developing a system that would help the RAF if the war should come. The details are, classified beyond our control, held by the Ministry of Defence.

John-Smith Patten asked if they had an address for him. Carter handed them the contact detail stating that he had lodgings in Blenheim Road off West Parade, number 21, but the tenants wouldn't return until the day after tomorrow. "What about his place of work", asked Munroe "Mostly he was working at Ruston-Bucyrus, the Institute of Mechanical Engineers. Other times he spends a lot of time at RAF Scamptom. Find out what happened if anything did happen to him then report back. Before Munroe left the room he turned then asked "what's his name" DCI Carter looked up from his paper work, Professor Isaacs Richard Churchill, "any relation then" remarked Munroe. A cousin twice removed.

Munroe and John-Smith Patten closed the door behind them and headed off down the corridor to their office. Munroe placed the file on his desk; walked over to the coffee pot poured himself a drink had a sip then dialled the met boys in London and to find out the phone number for the wife. Munroe dialled the phone number. After a few waiting moment's it started to ring.

"Hello" answered Mrs Churchill

"Mrs Churchill" enquired Munroe.

"Yes"

"It's DS Ray Munroe from Lincoln police" Munroe went on to explain that the case had been forwarded to them as her husband was working here, and that he required to speak to her. Munroe arranged the visit for tomorrow at noon. Placing the phone down he then dialled the number for St Mark's station, after a few minute a voice came on the line. Munroe wonted to know the next train to London. Tomorrow at 9.30am returning at 5 o'clock from Kings Cross, said the ticket man. Plenty of time thought Munroe. Ray passed the timings over to John-Smith. What now then asked John-Smith, Ray lifted his head from the folder then said, "It's time for home" They both got up from their chairs at the same time. Opening the office door, they noticed that DCI Carter was coming down the long corridor. Ray threw a small glace across at John-Smith indicating that here we go again. Surprised, as they were the DCI said good night and walked on.

Outside in the police car park Munroe noticed that it was still snowing heavy. "Wont a left then" John-Smith looked up towards the snow falling sky, and then turned his head towards his push bike covered in snow, walked the few steps to Munroe's car open the passage door got inside and waited for Munroe to start the engine. "I take that as a yes then," thought Munroe. The short journey to John-Smith home did not take them long. John-Smith ducked his head back in the car, "see you tomorrow then" "and thanks" then closed the door walked up the slippery hill towards Hillside Avenue turned the corner at the top then he was home. Munroe selected first gear easing the Ford along at a slow pace until the tyres had a better grip of the road. Turning the corner at the top of Greetwell Road Munroe witnessed a crash no one was hurt so continued home to Karan.

Pulling in the drive Munroe saw that the lights were still on. Closing his door Ray walked towards the yard gate. Duke was waiting on the other side; he had heard the sound of the Ford approaching barking to be, let out. Karen had laid the table for tea, stew was cooking on the stove, and it smelt well. After hanging, his coat up Munroe crossed the space to Karen. Placing his arms around her and at the same time kissing her slender neck, Karen squeezed his hands turned around to face him and then gave him a long and lasting kiss on the month. Releasing her grip on Munroe she, looked in his eyes and said that tea would be ready in 10 minutes. Making shore the stew was not; sticking Karen gently stirred the pan, and asked how the case was. Munroe brought Karan up to speed with what information he had. Karen looked at Ray when he mentioned that the science person name was Churchill. "Any relation then" said Karen. Munroe laughed then explained the joke.

With tea out of the way and the washing up done, the clock in the hall told them that it was only 8 O'clock at night, the night was still young, they both decided that they should wonder over for a quick pint before turning in for the night. Ray and Karen sat near the fire, Duke laid curled up in front of the fire. Most of the evening they talked and discussed Munroe's new case. Karen said she would find out what she could about this Professor Churchill. Closing time was Midnight. Munroe having to be up early to catch the train to London, so with good byes all around the Munroe's finally left the White Hart and made their way back home. Duke staggered along the snow, covered footpath after someone had spiked his water with drink it was not his first and it would not be his last.

4

The cold morning light creeped though the soft warm coloured texture curtains. Ray Munroe's alarm clock danced boldly around his side of the bed. Ray then felt Karen lean over his back to switch the button off. He could feel her rounded breasts pressed hard against the middle of his naked back. Turning back the bed covers, Karen noticed that his man hood was standing to attention. Without any words, Karen climbed over his legs and eased herself down slowly on his rock hard member, feeling the pleasure slid in side her with every inch. The stiffness of it made Karen hot and wet with each penetration it was not long before Karan climaxed with a loud scream of joy. Karen fell forward once Ray had climaxed, tighten her thighs around his legs to get the full pleasure from him before they both parted. Lying exhausted next to each other Ray turned his head and noticed that the clock, was telling him it was time to get up.

Munroe entering the kitchen noticed that Duke was still in his basket. He Duke managed to open one eye had a look at his master then closed it again, resting his hang over from the night before. Karen followed a few moments later wearing her dressing crown loosely tied up. Quick breakfast and it was time to pick up John-Smith. Munroe slid his hands through Karen's crown and kissed her tenderly placing his hand firmly on Karen left cheek bottom giving it a pat before he placed his hat on turned the kitchen door handle and walked out to the cold morning air. "See you later," Ray shouted.

John-Smith was standing on the pavement at the top of Roman Crescent banging his feet against the bitter cold wind trying to keep them warm. Looking to his left he finally saw

Munroe's Ford 10 sliding down the road towards him, only managing to stop in time. "Been waiting long" "long enough for my bloody feet to get cold" said John-Smith. Ray laughed then continued to the train station. Parking the car Ray looked upwards to the sky, it was full of snow. "Hope the trains on time," mentioned Ray. "As long as I can get a cuppa, it can do what it likes," said John-Smith heading off to the canteen before picking up the ticket to London. The train pulled in on time, sending columns of white smoke as it did so. Unlocking the first class carriage door both detectives entered, placing their hats and coats on the luggage rack above their seats they then settled down for the three-hour journey to Kings Cross station. Just out of the station, the ticket conductor arrived shouting "Tickets please". Producing their tickets, the conductor placed his whole punch through them. Now they had the peace and quiet for the rest of the journey.

The tan or system announcing the arrival of the train from Lincoln woke Munroe up. Peering out through the misty cold window Munroe noticed the amount of people moving about the platforms. The train eased forward to its resting place, leaning out the window John-Smith unlocked the carriage door and stepped on to the platform. Exiting the station Munroe hailed down a taxi that would take them to the address of Professor Churchill home.

Munroe arriving at the address paid the taxi driver then walked the tiny three steps to the front door, knocked twice and waited. Few minutes elapsed before the door was open by the butler. Both detectives showed their warrant cards, Munroe said they were here to see Mrs Churchill "please come in. I shall announce your presents to Mrs Churchill". Both waited in the lobby, which was of gilt-marble noticed Munroe. From the corner of his eye, Ray noticed movement on the stairs; glancing upwards, he noticed two young children. The boy was dressed in a navy outfit; the girl was wearing a pink dress with a white bow. Both children stared towards the detectives before speaking. The boy wanted to know why they had come. Ray said that they had come to speak with their Mummy, "what about my father" the girl who seemed older than the boy asked did. Munroe looked across at John-Smith before saying that they had not found him. Before the children could ask any more Questions the butler came back, he gave the children a glancing stare before, saying that Mrs Churchill would see them now.

Mrs Churchill was dressed stylishly with a vivacious gleam in her eyes. She was tall with a slim figure with flowing red hair a lot younger than Munroe was expecting. "Please gentlemen sit down; may I offer you a cup of Tea" Munroe said that would be kind. Ray watched her pour the tea out in a way that was proper and well educated in manners of entertaining others. Placing her napkin on her slender lap Mrs Churchill placed the cup of tea between her lips before she said anything to the detectives, glaring over the rim of the cup towards Munroe and John Smith. Placing the cup and saucer down gently she raised her eyes and stared at each detective in turn then said.

"So Detective Sargent Munroe, any news regarding my husband". Munroe shook his head from side to side. For a brief, second Ray let the motion of his movement stink in before he started to ask questions, Munroe watched Mrs Churchill reaction. Her expression did not change.

"Did you manage to speak to your husband before he was due home"? Mrs Churchill went silent for a moment before she answered, "He phoned the day before about 8 in the evening"

"How did he seem to you?"

“Well to be honest he sounded a bit down, in the dumps to be frank”

“What time and date was your husband due home”

“He was due to catch the early train from Lincoln back to Kings Cross on the 23rd” Once he did not show I called his office, they informed me that he had already left.

“What time was that?”

“Seven in the evening of the 23rd”. “Why did you leave phoning until that time?” asked Munroe. “My husband mentioned and told me that time when we spoke on the phone on the 22nd he said he had to meet someone at the train station so he might be late home,” informed Mrs Churchill.

Ray looked concerned, asked what the meaning of that time was to Mr Churchill. Mrs Churchill said “that her husband didn’t mention meaning of the time or the person name or why he had to meet him, he just told me to ring the office at that time, which I did” “I did not ask my husband what or who he was seeing.” Munroe went on to ask if Mrs Churchill ever questioned her husband’s actions on what he said. “No” was the answer. He has never explained why so I have never probe into the whys. Munroe felt sorry for her; here was an intelligent woman who had it all but imprisoned in the power of a husband and his work. Munroe also noticed that she was deeply in love with him.

“Can you remember his name?” The person you phoned. Asked Munroe

“A Mr Wightman-I think or it could be Right,” Munroe writing down the notes, said “is that spelt with an R or W” “with a W” she said. Munroe took his time in writing the notes down to have a look around the room. He noticed that she did not have any photos of her husband or of the children with in the room, strange to have a splendid room to look so empty.

"Just a few more question Mrs Churchill" said Munroe "Did you ever visit your husband in Lincoln?" Mrs Churchill went quite for a moment before she said "No", he said that his work was too important to have visitors" Mrs Churchill bowed her head lifting her napkin to her eyes after she had said that remark. Munroe could not help but to feel sorry for her, he felt that she could have done better, what a waste.
"What kind of work did your husband work in?"
Mrs Churchill cleared her throat by placing her hand over her mouth before she continued. "Am sorry but I have been told that I cannot give you that information" "But you do know what kind of work he was undertaking at Lincoln?" Mrs Churchill widens her lips to a smile, then said, "I do"
"Can you tell us who told you, you could not revile that information to us?"
"Yes I suppose I can- it was the Air Ministry" Munroe closed his notebook, with a thud.
"That confuses everyone,' Munroe explained with his warmest smile and a devilish glint in his eye. "Why" asked Mrs Churchill" It is typical of the incestuous relationship in the crowd of industrialists, Politicians, and diplomats that swirled around the 'Air Ministry' it's all down to them knowing and the rest of us trying to solve the mystery. "Is it a mystery?" said Mrs Churchill. "We haven't found your husband yet so it's a missing person enquiry for now. Munroe checked his watch it was time to go. They both stood up then Mrs Churchill rang the bell for the butler. Munroe walked towards her and gently shook her hand; it was warm and soft to the touch. Before we go, do you have a photo of Mr Churchill? Taken back with the request Mrs Churchill looked at her butler before indicating there should be one in Mr Churchill study. Leaving the drawing room door, open Munroe watched her cross the hall to the study room, closing

the door behind her, Ray through a glance at John – Smith in puzzlement. Moment later the door reopened, Mrs Churchill holding a photo in her left hand. Before she closed the door, Mrs Churchill lifted her head slightly and glared back into the study in a posture of eying someone who was in the room. Ray Munroe altered his gaze from the study, until Mrs Churchill handed the photo over. Munroe studied the photo socked to find the canny resemblance of the other Mr Churchill. Mrs Churchill smiled then said, "That the photo had been taken last year". Ray thanked her they would be in touch as soon as they had any information. With the photo in hand the detectives where let out by the butler. Standing on the second step Ray putting on his gloves mentioned to John-Smith if had seen the eye movement of Mrs Churchill before she closed the study door. John said he had. Walking some distance from the house Ray stopped, turned around and waited. "What going on" said John-Smith. "Wait and see"

They did not have long to wait until they both noticed the door being opened by the butler. A tall man wearing an over coat and gloves exited the Churchill residence. He shook Mrs Churchill's hand followed by a peck on her right cheek. The stranger turned the opposite way they hand done, given the stranger a few minutes' head start they then proceeded to followed.

John-Smith checked his watch it was three pm, plenty of time before the train left for Lincoln.

One hour later the stranger finally entered the building he was heading for. Walking passed Ray Munroe noticed that the building was the Air Ministry. Munroe reached into his coat pocket handed John-Smith a blank envelope. John-Smith looking puzzled wondering if Ray hand lost it turned and said "what" Walk in side and say that the gentleman who had just entered had dropped it" "and remember to find out his name" Munroe lighting up a cigarette carried on walking towards the bus stop and waited. John-Smith re-exited the building and hurried down the street towards Ray. Catching the number 10 bus to Kings Cross both Ray and John-Smith climbed the steps to the top deck. The seats were empty they were alone. "Well" said Ray. John-Smith explained that he had gone up to the reception, and handed the envelope over stating what Ray had said. The man behind the reception looked up when the brown envelope landed on the desk. The receptionist informed John-Smith that the envelope addressed for Mr George Edward Parker would be, passed on.

While John-Smith was heading out through the swing doors, Mr Parker started to descend the wooded stairs. The receptionist who handed over the package stopped him. Mr Parker looked bemused, opening the package he found that it contained nothing, turning he asked who had handed this over, "he didn't give his name sir" "never mind- thank you" He quickly ran to the open door to catch a final glimpse of Detective Sargent Ray Munroe walking on to the bus. "Very devious and clever" we shall meet again Ray Munroe said George Edward Parker, sooner than you think.

The journey back to Lincoln didn't take as long as it had coming to London thought Munroe, as soon as he had closed his eyes it was time to leave the train once the conductor had announced St Marks was the next stop. "What's the next step?" asked John-Smith "We'll make a visit to his lodging tomorrow" there is nothing more we can do to night. After dropping John-Smith off Munroe headed straight home to Karan.

Karan was out walking Duke when Ray parked the Ford; he noticed the note hanging on the rear Gate, stating that they would be doing the same route. He knew the route that was the same every night, taking them passed the Cathedral up to East Gate. Not bothering to get changed Munroe walked the opposite way to meet them both. Karen was dressed in her tweed over coat with matching trousers and hat; she looked beautiful with the evening sun shining it last rays on her. Duke was the first to notice his master, barking at Karen, who looked up saw Ray approaching then told Duke to go and find him. Mid way Duke stopped and looked back towards Karen making sure

That, she too was still following before he bounded up to Ray.

Ray Munroe hugged and kissed Karen passionately for a long time, holding each other Karan gazed into the eyes of Ray, "you look tired" "it's been a long day" How did you and John-Smith get on then? "I'll tell you all about it once we get home. Walking hand in hand, and with Duke at Ray's side they headed for home passing the White Hart pub on the way.

Seating by the open fire Ray told Karen all about the trip to London, the meeting with Mrs Churchill and of the stranger called Mr George Edward Parker. Karen turned her head facing Ray and said that Mr Parker was once a lawyer at the same firm as Karen had worked with. He had left for London about a year ago, never did say whom he was working with. "Could you dig around and find out what you can?" asked Ray. Karen smiled and said "it will cost you" but I shall do what I can. The clock above the fireplace chimed that it was time for bed. Letting Duke Out before he locked up Ray noticed that the snow had started to fall again, closing the cold night air out Munroe climbed the stairs with a smile on his face he had a payment to pay.

5

December 30th with more snow forecasted made Ray Munroe wrap up for the bitter cold wind. He headed out side to find the Ford covered, five minute after clearing the snow Munroe pulled out of his drive, windy down his window he gave a wave to Karen who was standing in the front room. Driving down the long road of Greetwell Road with the snowdrifts lying all along the kerbs Munroe finally eased the old Ford to a sliding stop. Ray looked down the slight hill leading of Roman Pavement and noticed though the glum of the falling snow John-Smith trudging along at a quick pace, not bothering to look up until he reached the main road. Munroe leaned over to open the passage door letting the cool air in cleaning the smell of cigarette smoke as it swirled around the interior of the Ford until the smoke found its escape route though the open window. "Morning" said John-Smith, Ray just nodded and smiled and then gently pulled away from the kerb, heading to Professor Churchill boarding house.

"What number was it?" asked Munroe. John-Smith checked his notebook, flickering though the endless page's he finally said "number 21". Outside number 21, Ray found that the tenants of number 21 had returned. Looking at the amount of snow on the roof, they had come back earlier than planned, thought Munroe parking behind. Ray looked up to the roof of number 21 counting how many windows represented rooms if any.

Easing his car door open Munroe adjusted his coat against the bitter winter wind before he opened the gate leading to the front door of number 21. The green door with its brass knocker stood proud. Knocking twice the door creaked open to a small elderly woman wearing clothing that could belong to any fine woman in society. "Good morning gentlemen, can I help you" Ray Munroe showed the elderly woman his warrant card. Taking back with surprise of the police on her doorstep, the elderly woman ushered both of them inside before the neighbourhood curtains started to peel back. "What's this all about officer?" said the woman. "Frist of all can we ask what your name is"? It is Mrs Mary Jane Wilson, "and your husband?" Richard Wilson. Mrs Wilson then showed them into the front room, Mr Wilson reading the paper when they entered, stood up when his wife announced that the police were here. Munroe told them both to sit down, and then went on to explain the purpose of the visit. Mrs Wilson went on to explain that Professor Churchill had been in lodgings with them for about six months, he paid his lodging in advance. Mrs Wilson said he was a very polite man charming in some ways. Always had a nice word to say. "Did he have many ladies' visit him?" asked Munroe. Mr Wilson said that he could recall one woman who had visited his room, very smartly dressed slim figure, flowing red hair stayed until way past midnight. "Are you sure about the description of this lady?" asked Munroe. "Quite" remarked Mr Wilson. "What date was this?" asked Munroe "It must be a week before Christmas round about the 18th – 19th" said Mr Wilson.

John-Smith asked if any other person had paid Mr Churchill a visit. Mrs Wilson looked towards Mr Wilson before answering. "After he had been here for a month or so a tall gentleman arrived asking for the professor, he was smartly dressed wore very expensive clothing as I can recall," said Mrs Wilson. "Did this person find Mr Churchill?" "No he was out for most of that day and returned late in the evening, banging his door which woke Mr Wilson from his sleep". Munroe could not help but chuckle to himself.

"When was the last date you both saw Mr Churchill?" stated Munroe. Mrs Wilson said, "It must have been the 23rd of December as they were packing the car to travel to York to visit their daughter, when the professor walked passed us". "Did he say anything? And was he carrying any luggage?" asked John-Smith. "He wished us both a merry Christmas then continued walking; he wasn't carrying any item of luggage not even his briefcase, which was strange as they had always seen him carrying it". "Which way was he walking when you saw him?" asked Munroe.

"Towards the train station" remarked Mr Wilson. "What time was this" "About 9.30" Munroe made a note of the time, then asked "After you last saw him at 9.30 did you then secure your house" Mr Wilson said that they made a swift look around to make sure the windows and doors had been closed before they finally closed the front door. "Was the door still shut when you arrived back," Asked John-Smith. Both the Wilson looked at each other, and then Mrs Wilson said that Mr Wilson re-opened the front door. The door was, still locked when he inserted the key if that is what you mean quizzed Mrs Wilson.

Munroe finished of writing his note then looked at both the Wilson. "Could you show us his room"? Mrs Wilson eased herself from the chair informing the detectives that she had to fetch the key from the kitchen, returning a few moments later with the spare key. Mr Churchill has his door key said Mrs Wilson, while walking towards the kitchen.

Climbing two flats of stairs Mrs Wilson stopped outside the second door on the right. Munroe glanced at the other door and remarked who rented it. Mrs Wilson lifted her head to look at Munroe, said that the room was empty, and had been for quite a while. Mrs Wilson inserted the room key but was having trouble pushing the key fully inwards. John-Smith had a try; still the key would not turn. Munroe asked if it was the right key. Mrs Wilson had a look of annoyance in the manner that implied that she did not know which key fitted which door turned her gaze away from Munroe and stared at the unlocked door. Munroe kneeled down and peeped through the key hole, what he saw was not what he was expecting. He stood up turned towards Mrs Wilson, then said, "The key is still inside the lock from the inside" Mrs Wilson placed her hands towards her cheeks in disbelief. "What are we to do now?" asked Mrs Wilson. Munroe said that they would have to force the door open with your permission of course. Mrs Wilson said that she would speak with her husband, keeping her gaze towards the door Mrs Wilson headed back down the stairs to find him.

After she had gone John-Smith looked at Munroe then said, "Can you smell that" sniffing the air as he said so. Ray Munroe moved closer to the door, sniffing it as he did so, and "It was coming from the inside". Five minute passed before both the Wilson came back. "Go ahead," said Mr Wilson. John-Smith placed his shoulder to the door and gave it a big push, it still would not move. "Try again with a bit more force" said Munroe. Finally, the door gave way to the force. Smell hit all four of them at the same time. The smell was of death Ray Munroe had come across before. He turned his head in the direction of the Wilson's he told them both to wait. John-Smith followed Munroe through the door to the darkness and smell. Finding the light switch the bright light brought the dark culmed eyrir, room to li

6

The detectives stood in silence for a few moments taken in the seen that was upon them. In the centre of the room suspended from the celling was the naked body of Professor Churchill he had been hanged, beneath his feet were the body waste which had been the cause of the smell along with the decomposing of his body. Both hands had, been tried behind his back. Munroe noticed the red markings were the rope had tightened. No other evidence of wrongdoing was evident upon his now lifeless body, apart from the gag around his mouth. The room was bare of all items of furniture all of it had been removed. Munroe quickly walked over to the windows trying to open them to let in fresh air. He noticed that even both the windows had been nailed shut and, with the room key left in the lock from the inside he wondered whoever did this must have been an artist in delusion - so how did he die? Moreover, why remove the furniture. How do you hang someone with no chair or table questions that Munroe hoped he would be able to find out? Meanwhile John-Smith hurried down the stairs to use the Wilson phone. Dialling the DCI's number, he quickly told him what he and Munroe had found. Munroe while he waited walked around the empty room looking at each wall trying to peace to together what had happened. On the joining wall to the next bedroom, Munroe noticed that the wallpaper had a slight stir along the centre, thinking no more about it Munroe waited until John-Smith returned.

After a period of time the sound of police, sirens could, be heard approaching the house of number 21. Munroe looked through the nailed down window which still had net curtains and noticed DCI Carter exit the first car, he did not look to happy. Uniform police started to cordon of the area. John-Smith opened the green door, letting DCI Carter into the Wilson front room where the Wilson where seating. Mr Wilson rose from his chair when he was informed who had entered the room, by John-Smith. DCI Carter walked over and shook his hand commentated that it was an awful thing finding Professor the way they had. The DCI walked back to the room door whispered to John-Smith, John-Smith told him the room was on the second floor, and nodded to the Wilson he then made his way up stairs to find Munroe. The smell started to drift down the stairs even before Carter found the room. Munroe was waiting outside the door when Carter stepped on to the landing. The DCI looked at Munroe then said, "You better show me what you have found" Ray Munroe stepped aside to let Carter in first. His first expression was to grab a hankie chief from his pocket placing it firmly around his mouth and noise. Walking around the body, he said "any chance of opening those windows" Munroe said that they had been nailed shut. Carter adverted his gaze away from the hanging lifeless body, withdrew the hankie way from his mouth and nose then said "break one then" Crashing glass could be heard coming though the floor boards. Both the Wilson raised their eyes up wards to the sound, then looked at John-Smith who said "that they had to break a window to let air into the room" Mr Wilson had a look at his wife who had started to cry, standing up he walked over to sit beside her, placing his arm around her shoulders for comfort. His eyes darted upwards to the ceiling he noticed a damp patch forming but took no further notice of it. Meanwhile upstairs, the DCI and Munroe now that fresh air was circulating discussed the cause of death. "Well what are your thoughts?" said the DCI to Munroe. Ray gazing out through the now broken window said "he was hanged because he knew some important scientific working's, or he did it himself" The DCI walked over to the window looked straight into Ray's eyes and said "what do you mean?" The evidence doesn't stand up to other people being in void, if they were how did they get out of a locked room" DCI Carter was about to comment when the forensic team arrived. Both men left the room letting the forensic team carry on with their work. Carter stopped outside the second room tried the door and found it to be, locked. "Do we know what's inside?" Ray Munroe told him that the Wilson said it had been empty for a while; "let's get a key and have a look," informed the DCI. Munroe went to the top of the stairs and told the PC to ask the Wilson to bring the key up.

Mrs Wilson slowly climbed the wooden stairs with the key, passed it over to DCI Carter and then started to proceed down stairs to re-join her husband. "What a minute" said the DCI? Unlocking the door, the DCI switched on the bear light bulb. What they found was a room full of furniture. However, what was more unusual was the amount of furniture. The room had two of every kind. Munroe stepped aside and beckoned Mrs Wilson over to show what he had found. Mrs Wilson entered the room both hands over her mouth in disbelief of what her eyes where telling her. She quickly stepped back from the sight bumping into Munroe. Ray caught her arm before she fell over. Turning around to face Munroe, he noticed that she was crying. "What has happened to us" enquired Mrs Wilson Ray placed a comforting arm round her and told her that what has been done is not her fault or your husband, before you go can you tell us which furniture belonged to Mr Churchill's room. Wiping away a tear she nodded then started to point and said "that all of it." One more question Mrs Wilson," said Munroe. "The key to this spare room, is that the only one"

“No the second key is still hanging up inside the larder room” “did your entire paying guest know there were spare keys? Mrs Wilson placed her arm on her hip stared hard and long at Munroe before she polity said” All my paying guest know there are two sets’ for each room both hanging on separate pegs.” Thank you said Munroe.

The room furniture neatly placed as it had been in the other room. Professor Churchill’s clothing was still hanging in the wardrobe as he had left it. The bed covers turned down for someone to climb in. Churchill’s suitcase lay on top of the wardrobe; it was if all the furniture was trying to tell Munroe something-but what? Ray searched amongst the endless furniture looking for the briefcase that Mrs Wilson had said he all ways carried with him. The briefcase had gone. DCI Carter told the forensic team to make a thorough check next door when they had finished. Nothing else here could be done until they had the report.

DCI Carter along with the Wilson drove back to the police station. The DCI told them it was “normal routine” and that they had to take a statement from both of you.

Outside in the cool afternoon winter’s day Ray Munroe a long with John-Smith shifted their coats firmly around their necks, before they started the door to door enquires. Ray started across the street from number 21; he had noticed that the front room curtain kept switching while he was upstairs. John-Smith started down the street towards the end.

Ray walked across the road and entered the small courtyard, knocked once on the heavy doorknocker the sound could be heard echoing form the inside. A very attractive young woman dressed in only her dressing robe holding it tightly against her chest opened the door with a beaming smile.

7

The beaming bright smile of the young woman changed when Munroe showed her his warrant card. Ray informed her why they were doing door the door enquiry is concerning the death of Professor Churchill. Opening the door wider the young woman showed Ray Munroe into her front room, the heat from the open fire hit Munroe like a fireball. Turning around he noticed that the woman was still standing on the front porch, coughing slightly the woman closed the front door behind her she took one more glancing look at the activity of what was happing in her quite world of caring for others. Munroe started by asking her name, "Miss Jean Isabella Wightman" she said. Ray looked across the room towards her, and then said, "Does your father work as a night watchman?" "Yes, how did you know?" Munroe went on to explain. "Where is your father now?" asked Munroe. Miss Jean went on to say that, her parents had gone away for Christmas to visit her sister's family in Newcastle, and would not be back until the New Year, round about the 3rd of January. Ray after taking notes rested his pencil had a look around the room then looked at Miss Jean before asking the provocative question of why she had not gone. Miss Jean said that she was a Nurse Sister and was on call at the Hospital until the New Year. Ray asked if she had seen any one, she had not recognised. Taking the question home firmly with in her mind, Miss Jean came back with two, which stood out. The first was a man aged round about his forty's, tall slim build wearing a long trench coat and hat which was always pulled down to cover his eyes." Did you witness this man often? Inquired Munroe. Miss Jean said that she had only seen him twice he always stopped outside number 21 for a few minutes, and always checked his watch, but never went in. Munroe looking puzzled asked how she had seen him while she was at the Hospital "Well said Miss Jean with another beaming smile, "The first time I saw him was when I was walking home from a night shift in the early morning, round about eight of the 20th. He was standing outside number 21, when I was crossed the road to his side he began to walk off in the opposite direction back up the road. I remember that he turned his head away from my direction when I started to cross the road so that I could not see his face; I thought that this was weird but thought nothing more of it. I watched him turn the corner before I went in. The, other time was when I was about to go on shift about two/three days from the first sighting. I was leaving the house as he was approaching number 21. Dressed the same as the first sighting again he checked his watch, but this time he dotted down something in a note book I thought it funny that I should see this stranger again so this time I called out if I could help. "What did he say?" asked Munroe? He looked straight across at me for a few seconds, did not say a word then continued walking down the street at a fast pace. It sent chives all over my body the way he looked at me. "Could you recognise him again in a line up? Miss Jean said she hoped she could. "Was that the last time you saw him?" Miss Jean redressed her robe that had fallen open, revelling her shapely curved legs before she answered, "It would be round about the 23rd it's the day I did a day shift" so yes that was the last time our paths crossed. "Did you see the Wilson loading their car up on the same day the 23rd? "Yes now you come to mention it they both wished me a happy Christmas the same time the stranger walked passed. "The Wilson did they have their back to the stranger when they were talking to you? “Yes” - “Why?” Said Miss Jean “Doesn’t matter” said Munroe, “And the other person you mentioned”. Said Munroe Miss Jean told him that it was a very smartly dressed woman, red hair slim body, very attractive. I was coming into my bedroom from having a bath and noticed her just entering number 21. I always leave my curtains open as my window overlooks the Wilson home. Mr Wilson let her in as I can recall.” What time did she leave?” asked Munroe. Well to be honest I was a bit nosey to tell you the truth as I kept on peeping though the open curtains waiting for her to leave. “And did you notice” “Um well I think it must be well after midnight as I was just about to go to bed when I heard the door open, I Always leave my bedroom window open for fresh air; the Wilson door makes an awful creaking sound when it is open.” When I looked through the window, I noticed they had started kissing. It went on for a very long time. Both stood on the porch before she finally said her good-bye. Mr Churchill stood and watched her walk away though the darkness of the night, the snow was falling so he watched her for a long time, even when she was out of sight he just stood on the porch he finally turned round and walked back inside closing the door wiping his eyes as he did so. I felt so sorry and sad for him. “Why” asked Munroe “Well it was like he was watching her go for the very last time and it seemed to me that he would not be seeing her again”. That was the only time that I saw her. “Can you remember the date?” Miss Jean said it might have been either the 17th-18th. “Is that the only time and date that, you saw this woman” asked Munroe and are you sure about the last date for the stranger being the 23rd? “Yes”-said Miss Jean

What about the professor Churchill? Did you often see him? Miss Jean said that she often walked with him when she was on day shift. He was a very charming person, always polite, and he all ways carried this old brown briefcase. "He told me that he was looking forward to going home for Christmas to be with his family". "When did he mention that to you?" asked Munroe. "Before I saw the lady arrive" After that visit he seemed withdrawn within himself very really wonting to talk about anything. He also told me that he would be back some time in the New Year. "When was the last time you saw him". Miss Jean stated that it must have been the 22nd the day before I saw the stranger, but not to talk too. "How did he seem to you on the 22nd" Miss Jean said that he looked like he was carrying the world on his shoulders. "Did he mention the kind of work he was carrying out?" said Munroe. Miss Jean stood up and walked over to the window peering through the net curtains; it had started to snow again. She noticed that the police were still doing the door-to-door enquiries. As she turned, Miss Jean saw that Ray Munroe had stood up and was looking at the photo of her parents that was, placed above the fireplace. Miss Jean approached Munroe, their arms torched for a brief second, Munroe realised what had happened and apologised. "Sorry it was my fault" said Miss Jean placing the photo back. "Your question concerning his work, he never mentioned it and I didn't bring the matter up". Miss Jean said.

Munroe wonted to know what Miss Jean was doing on the 24th 25th. "Both days I was on nights I came in round about 8.30 am then it was straight to bed until I woke up roundabout five. Most of the day I was in bed" she said. "Can you recall any sightings of anyone else over Christmas? Apart for the ones you have mentioned. Miss Jean told Munroe that apart from those that she had already mentioned she saw no one, the street was all empty, from the moment her parents had gone, even our neighbours had gone away, the residence that live here are old, there is one thou said Jean, a

Mr Dolek he lives next door to 21. He does not go out much always sits in the front room; I sometimes pop over to see him apart from him that is all I have seen. Munroe stood up and walked over to the fireplace glanced at the photo of Miss Jean parents turned around and said, "Your father was in the War I see?" changing the subject. Miss Jean placed her hands on her lap as if she was having a photo taken then informed Munroe that her father fought from 1914 to the end of the war; he was one of the lucky ones. He transferred to the tank battalion in the later part of the war. My father very really talks about those days, and I never ask. (Munroe smiled to himself, he would ask his father if he knew him.)

Ray Munroe stood up before he left he informed Miss Jean that she would have to make a statement in the police station in the next few days. Jean said she would call round when she was of shift. Miss Jean opened the leaving room door to show Ray Munroe out, holding the doorknob Jean turned and asked him "will you catch the man who did this". Ray stepped back looked in to Miss Jean's blue eyes then said "I shall" The front door let in the cool afternoon air which made Miss Jean shiver; she placed her arms tightly around her slender body for extra warmth. Across the street they both watched the lifeless body of Professor Churchill been carried down the few snow covered steps of number 21 to the waiting Vehicle. The Connery officers gently placed the body into the back closing the doors as quietly as not to wake the professor. The vehicle with its passenger slowly moved away leaving the place that once was his home. Jean had seen death before while at work, but this death was different she had known this person for a short while the reality of the situation was hard to understand, why someone had done this terrible thing.

Munroe was near to closing the yard gate when Miss Jean shouted; Ray turned and walked back towards her. "Almost forgot with a beaming smile," she said. "The stranger I remember had a slight limp" Which leg informed Munroe. "Left" Munroe touched his hat and turned around to walk through the gate. John-Smith noticed the woman with the robe a smile beaming on his face when he approached Munroe. "Not bad" said John-Smith nodding towards Miss Jean who was closing the door. "Very funny" said Munroe "How did you get on?" inquired Ray. John-Smith said that most of the neighbours had gone away apart from the couple at the top of the street. They did not see any one, so they say. "That leaves a Mr Dolek next door to the Wilsons then. Informed Munroe

The afternoon light was fading when they entered the home of Mr Dolek. Both detectives noticed that the man was wheel chair bound; he wore a row of medals from a war, which happened long before Munroe was born pinned to his broad chest.

The man seemed tall even thou he was in a wheel chair, clean-shaven and spoke with a deep sounding voice. A voice of an old man who had the meaning and had the authority, a time long ago now really used in his new word, which he called his front room. Mr Dolek indicated to the detective where to seat. Dolek was keen that they should keep the view open so he could see through the window. "Now what's going on?" asked the old man. Munroe told him of the gruesome finding of Professor Churchill. The old man looked out through the window in a moment of past memories of the times he had witnessed the professor walking past his home. He turned his sharp futures to look at Munroe, the look in his eyes that where filled with teardrops told their own story. He was sad at the death of a friend; he called him his friend even thou they never exchanged words, only by the rising of the arm each morning and evening did the friendship become part of the old man's daily existence. Munroe gave the old man a few moments to gather his thoughts before he stated his questions. Ray stood up and walked over towards the window, he was followed by the old operates eyes questioning the purpose of it all. Munroe looking both to the left and to right through the window taking in the view of what the old man could see turned around and said "Have you lived here long Mr Dolek?" The old man seating in his chair stopped twiddling his thumbs around, then said "my wife and I have been here for more years than I can remember" "Your wife is she around" "No she died some three years ago" "Am sorry to hear that said Munroe. Changing the subject Munroe went on to ask about his family. "The old man said that they two sons had both been lost to the last war, our daughter married now lives in Poland. Both sons have served with the Lincolnshire Regiment and both been killed during the battle of the Somme. My wife was heartbroken hearing the terrible news, I think that was the start of her end to live, mind you she lasted a further twenty years before her fight ended, said the old man. John-Smith was more interested about his medals and wonted to know which campaign he had fought though. The old man turned his head to look at John-Smith pointing to his medals. Bore War. Shot in the back that put me in this, indicating to the wheel chair. Munroe sensed his bitterness to his injury but left it alone. "How do you cope from day to day?" asked Munroe. "Next door, the Wilsons pop round most days to see if I need any food fetching, and Jean across the road she's always calling around, when she not on shift". Fine lass in many ways said the old man. "What do you mean?" inquired Munroe.

"The old man lifted out his pocket watch from his waste coat. John-Smith noticed it had an inscription on it. He flicked the catch then said "Look across the road at her house" Munroe looking through the net curtains noticed that her window was in direct line to where the old man sat. The street light had come on which was below her window, casting long shadows. Just then movement was, noticed inside her bedroom. Munroe kept his gaze firmly on the window; it was not long before Miss Jean came to the window frame completely naked. She stood there for a few breathing seconds showing the world her nakedness, straighten her arms high to lift her frim breast. When she had gone, Munroe turned around and said, "I see what you mean," laughing as he sat down. How did you know? She would do that. Inquired, Munro. The old man said that she does that routine most nights before she goes on shift, round about this time, looking at his clock "She knows that I look, am sure she does that to keep me going" laughed the old man. "Have you ever asked why she does that?" asked Munroe. The old man told both detectives that she enjoys walking around her bedroom with nothing on. "I bet when you talked to her she had nothing but a robe on. The old man said. Munroe smiled at John-Smith then said "that true"

The old man changed his expression his thought going back to his lost friend. Munroe asked him if he had seen any one that stood out from the 18th until the 23rd. The old man started with the stranger. He had seen him more times during that period than he had Jean. His routine the stranger was to walk up one side then walk down the other, always stopping outside number 21. What time where these asked John-Smith. The professor normally went to work round about seven in the morning and return any time after seven at night. On the other hand, the stranger changed his pattern from eight some mornings or arrive well after nine. “Did he seem to be waiting for the professor?” asked Munroe. The old man said, “Well if he did he didn’t make much about it” “What do you mean” “If I wanted to speak to him then I would have rung the doorbell –wouldn’t you?” answered the old man. Munroe smiled in the logic in the answer. John-Smith asked the old man if he could describe him. The old man looking out though his window, said that the stranger wore a large brown coat, hat pulled well down around his head the colour was black, gloves and he always had a Cigarette on the go. He did walk with a slight limp-his left leg. I did not really get a good look at his face. Jean saw more of his face than I. Munroe said that Miss Jean had already told him that. Anyone else that you can recall said John-Smith. The old man mentioned the young woman with following red hair she called round on the 18th and stayed for most of the night. Would you recognise her again if you saw her? The old man said he would always recognise a good-looking woman. Munroe handed over a photo to the old man. His eyes said it all. The woman in the black and white photo was the same person he had seen on the 18th. “Who is she” asked the old man. “It’s the professor’s wife,” Munroe said looking at John-smith. Was there anything else that might have stood out apart from those two? The old man thought hard and long then said “well on the 21st the professor came home early. It was not like him being home before seven, he was carrying a parcel that looked heavy, plus it looked wet- well the bottom of the cardboard box was. “Did he look your way when he passed?” asked Munroe. “Now that was strange said the old man, as he had always had a glance in my direction but this time he just walked by, straight into number 21. “What time was this?” asked Munroe. The old man looking at his watch then suddenly turned to look at Munroe, then said, “It was

three thirty on the dot" "How can you be so sure on the time?" inquired Munroe. The Wilson came round with a food hamper informing me that they would be away for Christmas; the doorbell rang on the stroke of three thirty. Munroe stood up again and walked to the window, glazing to the left then right. He turned to face the old man. "Do you sit in your chair were you are sitting now?" asked Munroe. The old man looked at John-Smith then moved his head towards Munroe. I sit were I am
Now why? Munroe came back and stood to the right of the old man, squatting down to the same height. Munroe wonted to see what the old man could see. To his right he could see roughly three houses down, but to the left he could see only two houses, one being Miss Jean house across the street. The old man had a blind spot caused by the telegraph pole outside number 21, any one approaching form the left, he could not see until they had passed the pole. "What's going on? "Asked the old Man. Munroe told him that where he sat he could see pity much of what the street was doing, but looking to the left you could not see any one until they passed the telegraph Pole. "So" said the old man. "Well the professor could have come back from the other direction or a person supposedly to be the professor could have entered number 21 and you would not be any the wiser" said Munroe. "Are you saying that this person I saw on the 23rd that had walked passed the Window wasn't the professor," asked the old man. Munroe eased himself up rubbing his legs then made his way to the chair alongside John-Smith. Munroe went on to say, "We think the professor might have died before the 23rd so you could have not seen who you thought you had seen on the 23rd. "But what about the Wilson? You said they saw him on the 23rd" That is right but again they did not have a good look as they were packing the

car, plus they both had their backs towards him. The Wilson all so said that he was not carrying any form of luggage or his brief case." The old man went slight absorbing the information that Munroe had just said. Both detectives stood up it was getting late, both noticed that the old man was looking tried. The old man stretched out his hand, he had tears in his eyes, and Munroe clasped both hands around his to give him reassurance before informing him that they would be in touch soon.

Once the detectives had left, the old man looking tried and drawn wheeled his chair around to the rear of the house. Standing in the shadow a tall figure leaned against the cupboard, he had heard what the old man had said. He blew out a long column of smoke that drifted slowly towards him. With one hand, the old man waved the smoke away from his face. The figure in the dark shadow was smiling.

8

Ray Munroe stepped through the open door of number 21. The bitter cold night air met him; it sucked what warmth he had from his body. John-Smith last to live closed Mr Dolek's door. Stopping alongside the Ford, Munroe turned to John-Smith with a questionable look. "What's your thought's John?" John-Smith placed his hands deep into his coat pockets for warmth stirred at Ray for a long minute before answering. "I believe that this, pointing up and down the street, is holding a dark secret there's more to this murder than we are able to understand at the moment. Munroe opening his door finally said "Let call it day, tomorrows New Year's Eve" On the way back to the station John-Smith was puzzled on how Ray had obtain a photo of Mrs Churchill. Munroe said that once he was handed the photo of the professor he noticed something white under the main photo, it was not until he reached home did he remove it and then he found a small photo of her. "Let's have a look." Munroe reached into his coat pocket and handed it over. John-Smith studied the photo, it looked like it was taken quite some time ago, "he said" and she looked a lot younger than she does now. The reverse side in hand written letters was "with love S.W.P". "Who is S.W.P" asked John-Smith. Munroe shrugged his shoulders then said, "I don't know –but I am going to find out".

Munroe eased the ford into his usual parking space, apart from his car the only other visible vehicle was that of the DCI. Entering the station, the duty sergeant greeted them by saying the DCI was waiting for them in his office. Munroe threw a quick glancing look towards John-Smith they then both walked the stairs to his office. After knocking on the door Munroe entered, the DCI was on the phone. With a wave of his hands, he indicated them to sit down. DCI Carter replaced the phone holding the hand set for a brief second before telling both detectives who was on the phone. The DCI informed them that it was Mr Churchill the First Lord of the Admiralty wanting to know the circumstances regarding the death of his cusion. "How did he find out so quickly?" asked John-Smith. Carter brought a slight smile to his lips and with the movement of his shoulders his answer was "Who knows" "Well Ray how did you get on" asked Carter. Munroe told him as far as the information they had gathered we are still none the wiser of how or why he was murdered. We still have no leads on who this stranger was or why he was constantly patrolling the street. We need to go back to number 21 for a closer look. Of the door-to-door enquiry's we still have to talk to the Station Commander at Scrampton the night watchman and the managing director where Churchill worked, those we cannot do until after the 4th of January. "That can wait," said Carter, first I have booked you a train ticket to London tomorrow at ten thirty to visit Mrs Churchill. Munroe new that he had to go but his idea was to take Karan with him and make a night of it; it was New Year's Eve after all. "By the way you can take your good lady with you," said Carter. Munro was about to ask the same question but just replied with "Thank you" After tiding up any lose ends both detectives headed back down to the car park

Munroe pulled the Ford over to a stop the same place he had picked John-Smith up, it seemed a long time ago, but in fact, it was only ten hours. Ray watched John-Smith battle with the wind and snow before he placed the Ford in first gear, his mind was darting back and forth with all the witness sightings of this so-called stranger who patrolled the street waiting for the right moment to strike his deadly blow to Professor Churchill. Unaware to Munroe this stranger would take him far beyond the shore's, of England.

Reaching home Munroe found Karen waiting, they both shared a lingering kiss; before Karen pulled away she looked hard into the face of Ray he looked drained and tired. "Hard day" asked
Karan. "You could say that, we found the body of Professor Churchill," said Munroe. "Was he Dead?" asked Karen. We found his body hung from the ceiling stated Ray. Munroe moved to the front room followed by Karen, sitting on the settee Munroe told Karen all about his day. When he had finished Karan leaned over and placed her arms around him, no words could endure the pain that befell the face of Ray Munroe." What's your next move" quizzed Karen? Munroe was about to answer when the phone started to ring. Munroe picking up the receiver listened to what the caller was staying, Munroe finished by answering he would be there. Who was that Karen wonted to know? Munroe turned round and said that it was the DCI, confirming the train timings for tomorrow to London for two passengers. Karen looked knowing her husband had the endless job to do, but New Year Eve of all days." Well you better get an early night's sleep then" quizzed Karan. Turning around she noticed that Ray had that smile that could have launched a thousand ships, "what's so funny". "Nothing really but the other ticket is for you" answered Munroe. Karen flung herself over towards Ray her arms around him and said "you, rotter".

Both Ray and Karen woke early; they both had the train to catch. Duke to be left at the White Hart; he had stayed before so was quite at home. Once they had said their good byes to Duke who was sitting in front of the fire. Ray and Karen moved to the door stepping outside, they noticed that the sun was breaking though it was quite warm for the middle of winter. Munroe opened the car door for Karen who looked at Ray with those gleaming bright eyes. She gilded her long and slender legs into the front well of the passenger seat, revelling her stockings held up by the suspender belt, an eye full for the on looker Harold, closing her door Ray walked behind the Ford to his door. He looked UP at Harold, who was standing on the steps, smiling at Karen “see you in a few days” said Munroe. Turning the Ford around in the old market square Munroe eased forward past the White Hart, Harold waved them good-bye, and he was still smiling. Slipping and sliding down the snowy Lindum Hill, they finally managed to pull up outside St Marks Station. Leaving the Ford in the station car park Ray and Karen headed straight onto the station platform. The wind whipped a fine mist of powdery snow through the almost empty station. Brightly reflecting particles of snow had scattered against the windows as if someone had placed them to reflect like diamonds through the glowing light of the open log burner that was cascading its light on them. Entering the ticket office Karen noticed a lone passenger sitting curled by the open fire. He looked up when they entered; a parting of the mouth reviled a small uninviting smile. Karen returned the smile; a look of wonderment fell on her face when Ray handed the tickets to her. “You okay”. Karen turned her gaze from the man then said, “I’ll tell you later” Moving her eyes in the direction of the man to indicate her concern. Munroe looked over her shoulder, the man was looking out through the patchily snow covered window then stood up and started to head in their direction. Munroe let out a cough to let Karen known that the man was approaching. “Gutter Morgan “said the stranger. Ray Munroe startled with the language placed his hand on to the rim of his hat then said “Good Morning”

Both the Munroe's watched the stranger leave the warmth of the ticket office only to stand on the platform looking in the direction of the train. The distance of the rising smoke told the passengers that the London train was coming. Through the gloom of the fine mist of snow, Karen witnessed the white smoke lifting its way clear out of the tall chimney parting its way through the endless snow that was falling. The sound of the engine whistle blowing informed the Munroe that the train was approaching the platform. Munroe picked the suitcase up and followed Karen out onto the cold platform. The hissing columns of white smoke covered the posture of Karan and Munroe. Once the smoke had cleared, they both entered the first class department, settling down for the long journey to London. Karen sat by the window watching the amount of snow, which was falling out side. Munroe placed

His suitcase on the luggage rack then sat down opposite Karen. "Well" said Munroe, Karen looked across at Munroe with the expression of knowing what the "well" meant. She started by saying that she got the impression that the stranger knew them, and knew that they would be entering the ticket office it was if he was waiting for us. "Did you see him climb abound the train?" Munroe thought about it for a while trying to put together the time they had entered the carriage if he had seen the stranger come aboard, now that Karan had mentioned it, he had not seen him. Munroe thought nothing more about the stranger. If he had, what happen next might have been avoided

Relaxing back in their seats, Munroe watched the station slowly pass them, before long all he could see was snow-covered fields. An hour into the journey Munroe got to his feet opened the carriage door and headed back to the second-class compartment, he told Karen to make sure the door was closed while he was gone. Not long after Munroe re-entered the department, no sign of the stranger was found anywhere on the train. Just then the train whistle sounded, Grantham station was coming into view.

Once the train had restarted its journey, the ticket conductor entered their department. "DS Munroe" he said. Munroe nodded he was then handed a telegraph without say another word closing the door behind him. Opening it, Munroe sat in silence taking in what he had read. "What wrong Ray." Munroe passed the telegraph over. **"Bomb gone off at St Mark's ticket office" stop. "No casualties" stop. "Phone station" stop. DC John-Smith** "What does this mean Ray?" asked Karan. Munroe looked at his wife for a short while before he finally said that they might have been the target for the bomber. "Who the stranger you think," asked Karan. Munroe shrugged his shoulders, and then said, "Did you see him leave any think or item behind, when he left the ticket office". Karen only mentioned that she thought she saw him drop his paper he was reading. Once the steam from the engine engulfed us on the platform, he might have done a runner out of the station. "But way blow up the ticket office an hour after we had gone, it doesn't make any sense" said Karen. "The only logic could be that the timer had been set wrong. Munroe thought about the case and the work Churchill was doing for the war office, could it be the Germans where by hide this, the stranger spoke with a German accent it was all too much of a coincidence. What he had to do was to notify John-Smith about his concern and about this so-called German stranger. The next due stop was Peterborough.

Before the train pulled into Peterborough Munroe left his carriage and headed off to find the train conductor. Explaining the circumstances relating to the bombing at Lincoln he told the conductor that he had to make a phone call as soon as the train pulled in. No sooner had the train come to a stop Munroe jumped off and made his way to the ticket office. Dialling the number, Munroe waited and waited until John-Smith picked up the receiver. Five minutes later Munroe was back on the train with Karen. “How did it go?” asked Karen. Munroe said the bomb had gone off as soon as we had left Lincoln. He does not have any further information, but would circulate the description of the stranger, we might get lucky but Munroe was not holding his breath.

9

Finally, the long train journey to London ended with the Lincoln train coming to a final stop. Ray and Karen Munroe stepped off the train on to the King Cross platform and walked the endless distance to the exit. Snow had started falling again in the capital, haling a taxi down they told the driver to head for the Dorchester Hotel. Munroe's father had bought them a penthouse suit, as a wedding present, some years ago. The Dorchester lobby was full of visitors ready to celebrate the New Year. Nearing the receptionist after gilding them, selves through the crowd, they soon booked in. The hotel bellhop carried their suitcase to the penthouse, a champagne bottle along with flowers sat on the main table in the middle of their room. Munroe turning around handed the bellhop a small tip, then closed the door. Ray walked over and used the penthouse phone to call the station. John-Smith picked up after the first ring. He informed Ray that a clock had been used to set off the bomb off had, been found. What was strange was the clock hands had been set for an hour after the train had left the station. The train, which they had boarded, had been the only one scheduled for that day. So the meaning of the bomb blast after the train had gone had baffled the DCI, it had served no purpose. Munroe listening to what John-Smith was saying, was in two minds, one was following what John-Smith was talking about the second part of his brain was remembering what he had said about the clock on the train with Karan. Interrupting John-Smith, he told him to find out what the time was in Germany. John-Smith baffled by what Munroe had asked for told Ray that the Germans were an hour ahead of us. "There you are then," said Munroe "What" said John-Smith. The stranger in the ticket office who spoke Germany is our bomber. Speak to the person who issued our ticket and find out if he had issued one to this stranger, or if they had spoken. Also, find out if any flight has taken of or is about to land from RAF Wickenby, destination Germany. John-Smith said he would call back within the next few hours. Munroe placed the handset he turned round to find Karen standing by the window watching the people moving in the direction of Trafalgar Square ready for the New Year celebrations. Ray moved closer to his wife wrapping his arms around her. He gently kissed her slender neck; she moved her shoulders high in the tender sensation of the caress giving her a tingling motion through her body. Karen placed her hand on his and quizzed them tightly in the, respire of what Ray was doing. Munroe moved his mouth to Karen's ear and wisped it was time to meet Mrs Churchill. Releasing his hold on Karen, Munroe walked to wards the bed collected their coats, helped Karen on with hers then they both made their way towards the hotel left.

Reaching the hotel lobby, which was still as packed, Munroe managed to catch the eye of the door attendant. Munroe asked him if he could hail a taxi for them. Opening the taxi door, the door attendant politely tipped his hat to Karen, nodded at Munroe with a smile then closed the door. The resident home of the Churchill's was a good thirty minutes away. Karen had time to explain on the way what she had managed to find out about the late professor Churchill. Munroe sat in silence, listening to what Karen was saying, before long the taxi pulled up outside the snow-covered home of the Churchill's.

Stepping up to the front door Munroe rang the outside bell, and waited. The Churchill's butler could, be heard approaching the door. The heavy door was soon opened,

“Good evening sir/madam” said the butler. Munroe produced his warrant card informing him that DS Munroe and Mrs Munroe requested to speak with Mrs Churchill. The butler opening the door wider showed them in to the entrance hall, closing the door behind them the butler informed them to wait. A few minutes later the butler appeared, with his out stretched arm he indicated that they should go into the drawing room.

Mrs Churchill was sitting by the large open fire gazing into the burning embers. When she noticed that both the Munroe has had entered, her grace and manor changed she sat up straight and with a slight smile welcomed them. “DS Munroe how nice to see you again” said Mrs Churchill. Munroe introduced his wife Karen. Munroe coughed before he started to tell his sad news on the death of Mr Churchill. Before he could speak, Mrs Churchill looked at Karan then at Munroe, tears started to form around her blue eyes, she knew that the news was not what she wanted to hear. “He’s dead isn’t he?” said Mrs Churchill. Karen rose from her chair and sat with Mrs Churchill; she gently placed her arm around her shoulders. Mrs Churchill turned her slender pale face to look at Karen. Karen gave Munroe a quick glance to tell him to continue. Munroe went on to outline the circumstance surrounding his death, leaving out the grim detail on how he was, found. Mrs Churchill bowed her head in a moment of pray then asked if her husband had died in pain. Munroe silent for a few moments said that they were still waiting on the medical report “What about witnesses” “We are still gathering information, on his last movements but with the festive season about us most people are away, so witness’s statement shall take time”. Munroe took a long deep sigh letting the death of her husband sink in before he continued with his questions.

Munroe noticed movement under the drawing room door that caught his eye. "Have you company to night, Mrs Churchill?" "No - why do you ask?" enquired Mrs Churchill. "Oh no matter" Munroe reached into his coat and retrieved the photo. Handing it over Munroe asked if the woman in the photo was of herself. Mrs Churchill gazing on the photo smiled then looked up and said. "No it's my darling twin sister". "Where in heavens did you find it?" asked Mrs Churchill. It was behind the photo you gave me of Mr Churchill. Mrs Churchill's expression changed to that of disbelief. "Really how very strange" remarked Mrs Churchill, who handed the photo back to Munroe. "Your sister does she live nearby" asked Munroe. Mrs Churchill rose from her seat then walked to the large bay window; gazing outside she noticed people walking pass ready to celebrate the New Year. The start of the New Year that will bring sadness to her family and a year of weariness' on what her future will bring. Mrs Churchill turned around facing both Ray and Karen. With her hands clasped in front of her, she told Munroe that her twin sister lived in a quite remote village in Cornwall. They had not seen each other for some time. Mrs Churchill went on to explain that they had a falling out a few years ago, since then they had not contacted each other. Munroe asked if Mr Churchill was in contact with her. "As far as I understand he was not," said Mrs Churchill. Munroe felt sorry for her, a woman who had given her all to a man who Munro thought was having a fare with her sister. The woman that Mr Kent and the Wilson has had seen, bothered him was it her sister or was it Mrs Churchill; Munroe started to drought his own mind.

Munroe asked if he could have her sister's address and telephone number, just to eliminate her from his enquiries. Mrs Churchill reached over for her address book found the page she was looking for then handed the book over to Munroe, who copied the address. Munroe noticed that her handwriting was slightly curved to one said. "Are you left handed Mrs Churchill" asked Munroe. Mrs Churchill lifted her gaze from the fire then looked at Karen, "Yes how did you know" "Just a hunch" said Munroe. "Your sister is she the same". Mrs Churchill said that both her sister and she were completely different when it came to doing things. Our parents had trouble telling us apart when we were so young, so they made us use different arms for doing things, such as writing and eating. My sister being right handed while I learnt to be left handed. Even during our school days, the teachers could not tell us apart, one teacher had the idea of tying different coloured ribbon in our hair, our father soon put a stop to that, laughed Mrs Churchill. Those were happy days, now they are but just a memory of what life was like. Does your sister live on her own? Mrs Churchill told them that her sister had never married she was too occupied with her work.

Munroe asked how she and Mr Churchill met. It was during our time at Oxford, we were both studying science. Over the years, our relationship became stronger, we finally married ten years ago, and we have been happy ever since.

Can you now tell me the nature of his work asked Munroe? Mrs Churchill looked again, at Karen; she wanted to see in Karan's eyes if she was doing the right thing, she was.

Mrs Churchill said that the, Air Ministry about a year ago approached him regarding the paper he was working on detecting aircraft using a system called radar. Radar is, used on an object detection system, which uses radio waves to determine the range, altitude direction or speed of the objects. Radar antenna transmits pulses of radio waves, which bounce off any object in their path. The objects return a tiny part of the wave's energy to an antenna that is usually located on the same site as the transmitter. This, system could be used for an early warning system. It is high tech and extremely secret. I was, told not to mention this to anyone. Munroe nodded his understanding; he let Mrs Churchill carry on. Antenna station where positioned around the white cliffs of Dover all linked together so that they over crossed each other. This gave the operator a bearing of the object. Is it in use or still on trial? The Air Ministry was so impressed that they have stated to install them. My husband had about four months' work to iron out the teething problems but the system was working. "You seem very well informed on his work?" said Karen. Mrs Churchill told them that they had worked together as both my husband and I have the same degree in science. "Did Mr Churchill give you any of his papers he was working on" He showed me his latest paper that did show a slight failure in the system. Mary informed them that her husband knew about it he hoped to complete in the New Year. Witness reports tell that he always carried a brief case. Mrs Churchill informed Munroe that the brief case was a present. Did Mr Churchill keep a second copy of his work? Asked Munroe. Mrs Churchill thought that if he had he would have left them secure at his place of work.

Ray Munroe checked the clock on top of the fire, place, it read 11.00 pm. It was time to leave. Karen stood up and clasped her hands in the palms of Mrs Churchill gently squeezing the soft tender hands. Both women looked into each other eyes, without saying any words they gently parted. Ray walked to the door before he had the chance to open it the door was, pushed inwards by the butler. Before he left the room Munroe tuned round to Mrs Churchill, one more question Mrs Churchill the initials S.W.A on the photo of your sister, what do they stand for? Mrs Churchill moved her eyes towards the fire before speaking, turning her gaze to Munroe she quietly said “Sybil with Affection”. Munroe looking puzzled asked the obvious question, “Why”. Mrs Churchill said that her sister had always finished of her letters with the letters S.W.A; it was her way of telling people that she cared. One more question, your sister, what kind of work does she do? Mrs Churchill went silent before she spoke; when she did, she told Munroe that her sister worked in a house for pleasure.

Munroe helped Karen on with her coat before the butler let in the cool night air. Turning each collar up against the cold wind Munroe and Karen turned around for on more look at Mrs Churchill. Her eyes had started to fill up with tears as she had the unquestionable task of informing her children on the death of their father. Karen could not help but to feel so sorry for her, in the sort time that they had been together Karen cloud feel that friendship might be in the making between them both. The door closed behind them leaving the Munroe’s standing on the doorsteps, leaving the warmth of the house behind them. The footpath coved in gleaming sparking snow looked inviting. “How long do we have” Karen asked. Not long, we had better hurry said Munroe.

Outside, the hotel, the snow came in thicker blasts and the wind pierced cold fingers through to the soul itself. In addition, far away to the East, the sky was blazed red with the glow of fires.

Four minutes to go said Munroe.

Every eye turned to the big clock above the window. No one spoke, all waiting in anticipation. Time dragged as the second hand on the clock seemed to take forever to make a sweep. Finally, Munroe spoke mechanically Happy New Year darling. Karen placing her arms around Ray’s neck drew him close for a deeply passionately kiss. Cheers filled the hotel bar, shake of hands could been seen going on all around the packed room, 1939 had arrived.

10

John-smith Patten replaced the receiver after Munroe had finished. He quickly phoned the duty Sargent requesting that a car should be ready to go to RAF Wickerby as soon as possible relating the urgency of the situation. Dialling the number for RAF Wickerby, John-Smith spoke to the duty Officer; he told John-Smith that a Heinkel He 70 was due to land within the next hour "Do you know who the passenger is". Asked John-Smith. A rustle of paper could be heard down the phone before the duty officer came back, his name is Friedrich Kessler, attaché form the German Embassy, and according to the time schedule, he should be here in a few minutes. John-Smith quite for a moment, then said, "Can you delay him until I arrive" "I can try". John-Smith replaced the phone, turning around he made his way to see the DCI. Carter stirring outside his window did not here his DC enter, until he looked round. "What wrong" John-Smith told him that the German was an attaché` for the German Embassy. DCI Cater jaw dropped, on hearing the news. He knew that all attaché had immunity when it came to English law; he had to make an urgent phone call to London. John-Smith headed down the stairs to the waiting car. RAF Wickerby lay roughly 10 miles out of Lincoln. The snow was falling hard and fast, which would make the journey longer, but he was determined to get to the airfield whatever the cost.

Reaching the guard post after what seemed an endless journey the duty Sargent approached the car when it pulled up, informing John-Smith that the Station Duty Officer FLT LT Townsend was waiting for him at air traffic control. Escorted by the RAF Police vehicle, John – Smith noticed that another vehicle was outside the control tower; its engine was still running. When both vehicles had stopped the duty, office stepped outside to greet DC John-Smith Pattern. Both shook hands, and at the same time tuned, and looked up towards the sound of an aircraft approaching the airfield. The duty officer said it was the Heinkel making its final approach. Stepping into the warmth of the tower John-Smith asked where Heir Kessler was. FLT LT Townsend said that they had put him the crew room. "Did you say anything to him"? "I told him that an incident had occurred at Lincoln train station and that a policeman was on his way".

John-Smith walked into the crew room. Kessler was watching the plane taxing towards the waiting marshal. Hearing the door creek, Kessler turned round. He was dressed in a full-length leather black coat, circular spectacles rested on his noise; under his left arm was a briefcase. John-Smith noticed that he was smoking a cigarette through a golden holder. Kessler clicked his heels together, followed by an out scratched hand. John-Smith walked closer, the handshake was frim. Kessler suddenly looked straight into the eyes of John-Smith with a glare of appraisal. He watched him for a few moments. There were years of shrewd experience and cunning behind his glance. Kessler broke his glance, then said, "How can I help you" John-Smith did not waste any time he asking him, if he was at Lincoln station this morning. Kessler relit his cigarette blowing out a long Colum of smoke, which drifted to the open window, before he came back with his answer. Kessler said that he was. He had just stepped of the train from London, then he realised that he was too early for his transport. Therefore, he decided to wait. John-Smith new that an early train had arrived from London before, but still asked what his purpose was here in Lincoln.

Blowing the last of the smoke and walking towards the window, Kessler mentioned that his work was to do with his Embassy and that he could not discuss it. With a slight turn of his head, Kessler smiled at John-Smith, he knew that any item relating to Embassy enrolment was questionable only to his own Embassy, not the English police.
Changing tactics John-Smith came back with the statement of the bomb explosion. Kessler face expression changed, he was not smiling any more. Looking out through the window Kessler asked if any one was hurt. Realising that he had shuck a nerve John-Smith told him that he knew of two who had Been, taken to the local hospital. “Who were they” asked Kessler. John-Smith with a slight smirk on his face informed him that it was DS Munroe and his wife. Kessler quickly turned round; his face was red, his eyes bulging from his sockets not believing what he heard. Just then, FLT LT Townsend knocked and entered. Townsend walked over whispered in John-Smith ear. Keeping his eyes firmly fixed on Kessler said, “that due to the weather condition the window of opportunity had arrived for your fight back to Germany.”” We shall continue this on your return Heir Kessler,” said John-Smith. Kessler walked slowly passed both men, he stopped in front of John-Smith smiled then said, “Our paths of life will cross again Heir Pattern” John-Smith waited until Kessler was near the door then said “Why did you decide to fly out of here Heir Kessler? Kessler stopped turned around, and then said, “It was Berlin that decided to use this airfield, not main”. The engine of the aircraft had started to turn over sending drifts of snow flying into the evening sky. The pilot was waiting for Heir Kessler. He came swiftly to attention then saluted moment later he too climbed aboard the waiting plane. Taxing to the edge of the runway the Heinkel waited for the clearance to take off. It was not long before

they were gathering speed, the rear wheel lifted from the tarmac of England for the last time. John-Smith kept watching until the aircraft was but a far distance spot in the evening sky. Flt Lt Townsend walked towards him, "strange that he said," What is" "the way that pilot saluted him, it was if he was an officer" "It must be his rank with the embassy" said John-Smith. May be may be not said Townsend, but I wager he was a high-ranking officer. By the way, we took some photos of him; once they are ready, I will send them on to you. John-Smith was about to follow when he turned and smelt a strong sent of cologne, had he smelt this before but where he could not remember. John-Smith eye then caught the sight of one of Kessler cigarette butts lying on the floor close to the window. Picking it up he noticed that it had a gold tip, placing it in his pocket John-Smith made his way out side to his waiting car. The other car with its engine running had gone.

Kessler relaxed in his seat after they had taken off from Wickerby. Reaching over to the adjoining seat Kessler took hold of the briefcase, unlocking the clasp he took the papers from the inside. Kessler placed his hands on the brown leather case, turned his head to gaze at the view of Lincoln then started to laugh.

Leaving RAF Wickerby far behind John-Smith with a beaming smile realised where he had first smelt that cologne. The jigsaw pieces were coming together.

11

Dawn spread slowly across the grey sky of London, bringing with it some respite from the agonizing weather. The snow had virtually stopped for a short rest bite and only the biting wind remained to chill the blood of man.

Karen woke early and not wanting to disturbed Ray, she gently eased herself out of the warmth of the bed. Tiptoeing her way to the large window, Karen drew open the curtains letting in the morning light to cascade over her naked body. Standing with her arms out stretched and still holding onto the curtains, she looked like a woman held together with the aid of only the fabric. Munroe turned over and feeling the empty pillow, released that Karen was not there, he turned his gaze towards the bright morning light entering though the window. Karen's body surrounded by the strong sunlight stood naked gazing on the enormous sight of London. Munroe walked over and gently clasped his hands around her middle moving them slowly upwards to her chest. Placing each warm hand over her breasts, feeling her already harden nipples. Karen moaned with the tingling sensation of what Ray was doing. He moved his hard throbbing manhood easily between her inner thighs. Still holding the curtains Karen started to bend slowly forward allowing Ray's manhood to enter her from the rear. His thrust was hard sending moans of pleasure echoing throughout the hotel. With the final thrust from Ray and of the morning sun, just breaking through they both climaxed, only then did Karen let go of the window curtains, to move her arms around Rays bottom to keep him inside her for as long as possible. Karen wanted this moment to last for a while longer.

Washed and changed Karen and Ray made their way down the winding stairs to the dining room. The waiter showed them their table, the same table they had always used. Breakfast soon followed. After breakfast, they decided to head off into the capital before the Lincoln train left Kings Cross. Both wrapped up for the chill wind Ray and Karen headed off. Almost at the same time that they had turned the corner from the hotel, a police car pulled up outside. The driver hurried inside only to emerge a few minutes later.

Strolling down the road hand in hand, Karen and Ray Munroe were unaware that they were being followed. Karan stopped to gaze into one of the big shop windows admiring the display of floral dresses. Through the reflection of the window, Munroe noticed that two men on the opposite side of the road had also stopped. Not looking around Munroe told Karen that he thought they had company, in the form of two men dressed with long over coats and hats pulled down to shield their eyes. Karan looked hard into the eyes of Ray wanting to know what they should do. Munroe smiled at his wife then trendily kissed her, took hold of her hand and headed off further down the road. At the next shop window, Munroe noticed that the company was still on the opposite side. Just then, the sound of a siren could be heard approaching at speed. Munroe looked across the street at the two men. Once the siren was heard, the two men quickly vanished. The police car pulled over to where Karen and Ray Munroe had stopped. Opening his door, the police constable walked up to Munroe, stopping long enough to inform them that his Chief Constable wanted to speak with them ungentle. Stepping into the police car the driver soon had them outside Scotland Yard. Walking towards the main entrance, the door was, opened by the duty sergeant. A large smile on the sergeant face greeted them both. “DS Munro” asked the sergeant. "Yes" "Follow me please the CC is waiting for you". Walking up the flight of stairs Karen held on to Ray's hand. He gently squeezed her hand as they neared the door. The sergeant knocked once, a loud response echoed through the soled door. On entering they both noticed three men where positioned around the main table. Karen recognised that one of the men was George Edward Parker; she quickly turned her head and looked at Ray. Ray gave a slight nod in response.

Chief Constable Martin came from behind his desk extending his hand. He introduced himself and the other two men. The third man was, only introduced as Dalton. Parker followed suit and gave Munroe a firm handshake. Clasping Karen hands, he bent slowly forward and kissed her softly on both cheeks. "It's been a while Karen" said Parker. Karen smiled and simply said, "It has".

Chief Constable Martin cleared his throat then said, "I have spoken with your DI in Lincoln on, your investigation over the death of Professor Churchill and of the bombing of the ticket office at ST Mark's station. He also said that you are still waiting for the medical report" "that right sir" Are you aware of what this Churchill fellow was doing for the Air Ministry. With a slight pause and a Quick look at Karen, Munroe answered. "I wasn't at the time of the death. However, after speaking with Mrs Churchill yesterday, she told us the nature of his work. "Why"? Martin was about to answer when Dalton stood up to explain. He began by saying, that due to the unstable state in Germany and the probability of war, looming over the channel with the impending invasion of Poland. It had been decided that this country needs a head start in safe, guarding our island. That's, how Professor Churchill came into this. For a long time, he had produced a paper on radar. Within our government it was, agreed for him to start his work, as soon as possible. Due to the high security and the nature of his work, working with the Royal Air Force. We felt it would be better if he stayed in a Bed and breakfast establishment, not wanting to arouse any suspicions. Not long after his work started, my department was, informed that the Germanys had sent over a very highly trained individual. His field of expertness' was radar. His name, Heir Friedrich Kessler who I might add you both met at Lincoln ticket office. The thought of him in the ticket office sent a Shiver through Karen's body. Highly decorated and educated in science and a personnel friend of Hitler he was the ideal man for the job. In Hitler's Germany, laws are now being, passed to discriminate viciously against Jews while teachers, doctors and lawyers are being, bullied into joining the Nazi party. That last statement concerning Jews has some relevance in the death of our professor. We are certain that he had to have had help, from someone in the same street relayed vital information to Kessler. Munroe wanted to know how long this Kessler had been roaming the streets of Lincoln, and why he had not been arrested. Dalton turned to Martin before he answered; a nod of the head told him he could answer the question. Professor Churchill new the risk he was undertaking it was all a plot by us so for the Germans to gather the wrong information. "So what wrong," asked Karan. They found out that our deception plan was a plot masterminded by us. "From who" enquired Munroe? Martin took over. "That's where you come in Munroe. As we have said, the mole is someone down that street who we do not know". Karen stood up looked at the three men, and then said, "You all let an ignorance man die for a worthless bit of paper why?" Parker the lawyer was the next to speak, he had been quite all the way though, up to now. He told them that they wonted Kessler to be, as they say flushed out and the only way that this could work was by this deception plan. He had been involved in the torcher and murder of one of our agents sent over to Germany. For some time, Germany has been building an early warning system, not to from that of our own. His mission was to find out what he could and report back, he never did. As soon as his feet had reached Germany, they had him arrested and, imprisoned. Kessler himself conducted the integration it took him a month to gather the information he wonted about Professor Churchill before he had the agent shot. Munroe still could not get his head around why they had Churchill involved in this. Dalton told them that Churchill's radar had already, been invented and was working. Why he became involved was because the agent was his stepbrother. "And Mrs Churchill, did she know what was going on" asked Karen. Dalton looked at her closed his eyes then said "She did" Munroe stood up taking in what the three men had said. "So what you are saying is that the death that was not met to happen, did happen and Kessler got away with it. Can you explain to us then what was the purpose of it all"? Martin walked over to his window, hands behind his back. He did Not speak for a while when he did it was full of sorrow. He slowly turned around and faced the room. "Our enrolment in this enquiry was to catch a spy and to safe guard our country, we (he looked at Parker and Dalton) have let this nation down. What we have to do now is apprehend the person responsible for this and to bring him or them to justice. In addition, for the record both the Churchill's new the risk that they were undertaking. Karen looked at Parker she wanted to know what his involvement was. Parker started by saying once he left Lincoln he joined a group of solicitors working for the Government. The cases concerning the Churchill's where passed to me; I was solely responsible for any imprecation relating to the case. As it has turned out it has become more complicated than I expected, due to his death. “You mean Murder,” said Karen. “That’s unfair none of us knew what was to happen”. A moment of silence filled the room before Munroe spoke. He turned to Dalton his question was blunt and to the point, “those two men who were following us, were they yours”? Dalton startled by the question replied without any hesitation that they were not his men. Dalton believed that Kessler did not kill Mr Churchill, as he was in London from the 20th until the day you saw him in Lincoln. There for, along with the in format in Lincoln I be leave he had another person stalking the Professor, and I be leave he is the one who killed him. “So why have us followed,” questioned Karen. “They whoever they might be think that you two know more about this case and the work that Churchill was doing. If they can gather what information they can from you, they will what the outcome might be. Munroe stood up and said “Kessler, if I am right in thinking he has all the information he needs in that briefcase he took so why bother us?” There is still a second copy of his notes. They who are following you believe that you will lead them to it. Without the second copy, the radar can be, altered in our favour. Regardless.

Dalton for a few seconds looked at the Chief Constable. What he was about to say was so highly secret only a hand full of people new. “When we knew that Kessler was heading to Lincoln to pick up the brief case we had him tailed and then we just watched and waited, but lost him before we could see who handed over the briefcase. The next time we had a sighting about him was at the station Your DC John-Smith spoiled it somewhat your DI will tell you more. In the end, the only option we had was for us to stop him getting away at any cost. “What are you saying” Munroe asked. Over the English Channel, two Gloster Gladiators shot down the plane Kessler was travelling in. No survivors. "And the brief case" As far as we know it went down with the plane, again we had no sighting of any wreckage. Either by air or from the sea.

So what now asked Munroe? Martin came from behind his desk, now you continue with your investigation and find out who did this, and find that second copy. Dalton looked at Karen then at Munroe if you need my help please phone this number, handing a card to Munroe.

Martin opened his office door to let Karen and Ray Munroe out, nothing more was said. Martin shook both their hands and told Munroe that his car would be outside, to take them back to their hotel. Before he left Munroe turned around and had a last look at the three men.

Far out in middle of the English, channel bubbles started to rise from the cold, dark gloomy depths. With a finally hiss the wet sodden brief case surfaced.

12

Munroe checked the timing they had a few minutes to wait until the train pulled in. Karen noticed a small café that was still open. Seating outside the waiter took their order, few seconds later the steaming cups of tea arrived. Munroe pulled out his cigarettes packet, handed one to Karen. Both sat in silence for a while until Karen broke the ice. “What are you thinking about?” asked Karen? Munroe looking over the rim of his cup smiled placed the cup down and reached over to hold Karen’s hand. He held it firmly with tenderness. When he realised it Ray said, “He was thinking of what had happened in the last few hours” He turned his head towards the approaching train. White smoke was bellowing out through its tall chimney. With a finally hiss from its brake’s the Lincoln train came to a halt. Karen and Ray walked hand in hand towards the first class carriage department. Placing the luggage on the rack above the seat, they settled down for the long journey home. Karen placed her head on Ray’s shoulder and soon fell fast asleep, as the gently movement of the train left the platform. The landscape out of London, blanketed in white snow, the sun was shining it last rays of warmth before it finally disappeared. In the far distance hill’s a few sheep where grazing beneath the snow looking for grass. The clouds turned from white to cold dark clouds it was turning cold again.

The journey through the snow-covered landscape towards Lincoln was long. Colum’s of white smoke drifting endlessly pasted the carriage windows to the rear of the train only to be lifted high into the dark unwelcome sky. Karen woke to notice that Munroe was staring out of the carriage window into the dark moonless night. "What wrong Ray" she asked. Ray turned his head to look at Karen. His features were that of a man who had the world on his shoulders. "Nothing darling just trying to piece together what was said to us" nothing to worry about.

The train whistle blew to announce that the train from London was pulling into St Mark's station. Both Ray and Karen eagerly stared out through the carriage window to get a better view of the shattered ticket office. The station was almost empty when the Munroe's stepped onto the cold platform it felt like a ere place to stand and view what the bomb blast had done. Left was a stack of scorched planks and bricks that was once the vocal point of the station. It would, be rebuilt to its old grand design. Holding hands, they exited the platform to find their car covered in snow. Working together, along with a snowball fight they soon had it cleared and were on their way to the pub to pick up Duke. Before they reached the pub, and without looking at Karen, Munroe said, "tomorrow he would invite Mrs Churchill down to stay", Karen was stunned by the last statement which came out of the blue looked at Munroe her expression on her face was full of "why". Munroe stopped alongside the Cathedral, turned towards Karen then started to explain. "When we asked the question did the Churchill's know what was going on, they told us they did. But when we asked Mrs Churchill when she was on her own, she denied it why?" "I still feel that the whole story has not reached the service yet, and why shoot down an unarmed plane. They knew that Kessler did not have the right papers, it doesn't make any sense." It has all been one hell of fuck up from the start "I thought Dalton said that Kessler had had the main papers". "No he had the copy, that's why they want us to find the original," said Munroe. Karen sat and stared out though the car window. Not looking at Ray, she simply said "Great"

After thanking, Harold Karen decided to walk the small distance home with Duke. Munroe drove on and finally pulled into the drive. Stepping on to the white crisp snow Ray walked to wards the rear gate. He could not help to notice that another set of footprint had also walked to the gate. Munroe Looked behind him his eyes followed the tracks, they stopped dead just before the road. Strange he thought that he did not notice any other car tracks or footprints when he had turned the corner. His mind was racing ahead. Munroe quietly opened the gate, with a slight push the gate opened due to the build-up of snow. The yard and rear garden was full of white virgin snow, not even a bird had left its mark deep in the crisp snow. The footprints again stopped abruptly at the gate, had they heard Munroe approaching and then turned away, thought and a reprehension had told Munroe that whoever made these Prints, knew were we lived. Just then, Ray head the familiar sound of Duke bounding towards him, followed closely by Karen. Munroe turned away from the garden and walked to meet Karen. Duke kept barking all the way, until he was with his master. "Strange" said Karen when she was at earshot from Munroe. "What Was?" "This stranger, a tall dark middle age person dancing alone the gutter, while whistling a tune. The melody was mournful, reminiscent of a faraway Scottish piper" He had a golden head of hair, strange that he was not wearing a hat of some sort. His clothes looked like they had, been slept in. Like handouts' from a church or lifted from a clothesline. He bumped into a lamppost and lost the thread of his whistle, and then he had gone. Munroe looked down the road in the direction Karen had walked home. Following his car tyres, he could just make out footprints in between the tracks left by his car, leading to the yard gate. Karen walked up to him, placed her arm through his looked into his eyes then said "What's wrong" Munroe gave Karen a friendly smile, pointed to the footprints, then said. "We have had visitors". Karen followed the direction Munroe was making with his arm. When she followed the prints to the yard gate, she clung on harder to Rays arm. "Who's prints are they?" asked Karen. Suddenly Duke started to bark; both Karen and Ray turned around moved from the road and walked the short distance towards Duke.

Munroe unlocked the door, the house felt cold and empty. Karen went into the front room to light the fire; it was not long before warmth started to filter through the house. Just then, the phone rang, walking to pick up the receiver Karen shouted that she was off for a bath. Munroe answered, it was John-Smith welcoming them back. He told Munroe about his encounter with Kessler but would bring him up to date tomorrow. Ray told him he would pick him up for eight in the morning. After placing, the receiver down Munroe dialled the number for the Manor, the Brigadier answered. Ray quickly told him about the professor and of Mrs Churchill staying with them. His father placed the phone down then walked into the drawing room to tell Elizabeth that they would be having a guess staying for a while.

Ray made sure the door was closed and locked, and then went upstairs. Karen was lying with her eyes closed when Munroe entered the bathroom. He sat on the edge of the bath admiring the burette of Karen. She opened her eyes when he started to tell her that he had phoned the Manor concerning Mrs Churchill. Her smile was warm and inviting, Karen handed Munroe the soap then sat up. The water cascaded down her neck over her pink nipples sending tiny droplets of bath water splashing between her thighs. The ripples moved her pubic hair almost as if they were blowing in a breeze. Moments of silence filled the room before Karen asked the concerning question, “Who was that man” Ray placed a hand on her left shoulder he wanted to make her feel safe but new that whoever the man was lived in Lincoln. “Remember what the Chief Constable Martin said that they thought Kessler had help here in Lincoln, well that could have been him” said Munroe. Karen stood up letting the water, cascade from her naked body. Ray handed her a towel, clasping it around her tightly, Karen stepped out from the bath. She desperately tried to hold the towel together at the same time placing her arms around Munroe’s neck. The towel slowly slipped down to the wet floor. Munroe gently lifted her and went through to the bedroom. Still kissing tenderly, they fell together on the soft warm bed. The heat from the open fireplace in the bedroom soon dried her naked body. Karen undressed Ray quickly their love making lasted well into the night.

13

Ray woke early to the sound of barking. Turning over he realised that the time was nearly 6.30am. Karen placed her arm across Ray's chest. With a morning kiss to Karen, Munroe eased himself out of bed. Down stairs Duke was still barking, something or someone was making him unease. Munroe opened the curtains the snow had stopped. Bright sky was, seen creeping up wards from the east. Duke bounded up the garden to the fence, sniffed once then carried on as if he was sensing something had entered his world. Munroe looked around the snow that had not been marked by Duke. No footprints were visible. Closing the door Ray moved back towards the kitchen, he switched the kettle on. Karen walked down stairs towards him; her robe was open revelling her naked body. The cold cool air from outside soon made Karen's nipples hard. Ray noticed the sudden change in her. She was proud of the way she looked and enjoyed walking around without any clothes on. She sensed that she was free when she had nothing on. Munroe placed his hands around her gently passing his hands over her breasts to bring Karen close they embraced for a while before the kettle whistled.

Dressed and ready Munroe left Karen behind telling her to remember to phone Mrs Churchill. John-Smith Patten waited patiently for the arrival of Ray Munroe. He saw the Ford slowly creeping towards him, sapping out his cigarette John-Smith placed his cold hands deep inside his coat pockets. Munroe pulled over to let John-Smith in. Both wished each other a happy New Year, and then it was down to business.

Sliding to a gentle stop outside the police station, Munroe and John-Smith walked the short distance to the main entrance. DCI Carter followed them in, "Morning Munroe and Patterson" both detectives looked at each other followed by "Morning Sir". The office was cold when Munroe entered looking around he soon found the switch for the heater. John-Smith went straight to his desk. A large brown envelope sat waiting for it to be open. Munroe looked up from his desk peering at what John-Smith was doing. "That report on the station ticket officer what did he have to say?" John-Smith retrieved it form a mile of paper work. "He said that once the London train had stopped only one passenger stepped off. The description given was that he was wearing a large black coat with hat and wore circular rimmed glasses. When he entered, he only asked if he could wait, as his transport was late. Kessler mentioned the same when I questioned him at RAF Wickerby said John – Smith. Not long after another stranger wearing, the same black coat arrived. The ticket officer remembered that this man was carrying a brief case and a parcel wrapped up and tied with string, and that he walked with a slight limp on his left leg "Did this second man say anything?" asked Munroe. No just nodded his head in his direction then sat down and started talking to the other man. "How long were they talking for" He couldn't remember as soon as they had started talking he went in the back to make himself a brew, when he returned the only man left in the station was the second man. Where the other one had gone he does not know. "What about the brief case and parcel?" Again, he could not remember seeing it or not. The next thing he remembers is when you and Karen walked in and the other stranger leaving. "What time was the London train" About thirty minutes before you arrived for your train. "Why" Specking out, loud Munroe said, "They had plenty of time once the ticket officer went into the rear to plant the bomb". John-Smith walked over to Munroe carrying the envelope. "What's this then?" asked Munroe. When I was talking to the RAF officer, he mentioned that they had taken some photos of Kessler. Munroe studied closely at the photos before John-Smith asked if that was the man, he had seen at the station office. Ray lifted his eyes to John-Smith. With a shake of his head, he told John-Smith that it was not the same man he had seen at the ticket office. Just then, the duty sergeant walked in carrying the medical report on Professor Churchill. Munroe quickly flicked though it stopping at the cause of death. Silence befell the office it was as if they were in church. Not a needle dropping or sound could be, heard. The report made interesting reading, but at the same time, it brought home what the Professor had gone though. The medical officer confirmed that the cause was from strangulation but also reported that it would have been a very slow and anguishing Death lasting few hours, if not days. A small amount of wading found lodged in his mouth preventing him from calling out. The damaging report was that this man was tortured before the rope placed around his neck. The way that he was tortured brought tears to Munroe's eyes. Professor Churchill had been injected with a very small amount of acid into his testicles the pain would have been unbearable, but according to the medical report not enough to kill him out right. He also read that the professor's scrotum had been stitched up. Both his testicles had been removed through the skin by hand. Skin particles and blood had been found under the professor's fingernails of the right hand indicating that he had ripped them out himself with conceivable force. Without the stitching and tiring of the blood flow-taking place the professor would have bled to death, the amount of blood lost would have been evident at the scene. In addition, he had a small puncher wound to both inner ears; this was done a while after the torture had taken place, disabling the professor form hearing according to the medical report. Estimated time the professor had to endure this torture was between two and three days. Ray's mind was trying to pitch together the seen, which he had just read. The professor must have managed to get his hand free to carry out what he did. His mind must have been on relieving the pain he was going through, instead of trying to escape and in the hope that this action would end his torment. The last paragraph of the medical report puzzled Munroe. He mentioned that further examination of the body found that both feet had the early stages of frostbite. No other expiration had been written down. Munroe placed the folder down resting his hands together, and then looked over at John-Smith. "You better read this," said Munroe. John-Smith walked over to his own desk before he started to read it. A few moments later John-Smith looking pale then said, "So where was this torture carried out?" Munroe got up from behind his desk and started to pace around the office before he stopped turned around and said, "I think it was carried out in his own bedroom before he was hanged" How when no furniture was in his room. Easily it was done, before the room was empty. Professor Churchill by this time would have been unconscious though all the pain and blood lost he had suffered so who ever had carried this out would have had time to move the furniture and carry out the hanging. What we have to do now is solve how this was done.

Munroe grabbing his coat, and hat and started to exit the office when John-smith piped up and asked, "Where are you going?" Back to the Wilson place.

Parking outside Number 21 Ray noticed that the neighbourhood curtains had started to switch as soon as they had moved down the street. Knocking a rat, a tat on the front door the detectives waited. Mrs Wilson with a beaming smile opened the door. Munroe removed his hat before stepping inside. "How can I help?" inquired Mrs Wilson. We like to have another look at the rooms, if that is okay with you. Mrs Wilson moved her head, a quick look at Mr Wilson before nodding her head. "Thank you". Said Munroe

Climbing the creaking stairs to the first landing, John-Smith could still smell the same smell that they had first come across when they had entered the room of Professor Churchill. He made a small cough Munroe turned his head in response. Turning the handle into the bedroom both detectives noticed that the room was the same as they had first seen it, apart from the body. Munroe walked into the centre of the room. He stood at the spot where the Professor had died. Ray turned his body in a 360 degree taking in in what he saw. His gaze stopped at the adjoining wall. Something was wrong in the way the wallpaper had been hung. Stepping closer he ran his fingers across the joins. His hand stopped when he felt a slight rise in the wall. Reaching inside his coat, he withdrew his penknife and slowly peeled back the paper. What he found was a new panel different in colour and texture from the rest of the wall. John-Smith walked over and stood by Munroe's side. Prising the Knife in-between, the joins he found that the new panel came away easily revealing a large opening leading through into the adjoining room. The panel was blocked by the large wardrobe. John-Smith turned and went next door. He quickly pushed the heavy wardrobe out of the way. Ray Munroe was standing smiling though the panel. "So that's how it was done," said John-Smith. Nevertheless, why do all this instead of taking the furniture through the door. It was easier for him to go through the wall than it would have been manoeuvring all the furniture through both doors and the corridor. "But why go to all this" said John-Smith. Munroe gazed at the amount of work it had taken in Matching up the wallpaper and making the false panel. Without that slight mistake they would not have been any the wiser. "To answer your question in why. It is simple. Who ever thought of this wonted us to consecrate purely on how the Professor had been hanged, that part we still do not understand. Munroe stepped through the opening. His eyes focused on the second bed. Turning *back the covers both detectives noticed a dark stain on the mattress. John-Smith lifted the side* nearest to him what they found was a larger stain of dry blood-they had found were the Professor had been tortured. "That explains the blood lost then," said John-Smith. Munroe walked back through the opening. He turned then asked John-Smith where the bed had been according to Mrs Wilson. John-Smith whipped through the pages of his notebook, "on the wall which we had just uncovered" said John-Smith. Checking the floor boards Munroe noticed that a small discolouring in two parts of the floor boards where evident. The first discolouring would have been under the bed if the bed were in the room. Munroe told John-Smith to fetch a crow bar from the Wilson's. In the meantime, Ray Munroe walked over to the window. Looking across the street he saw that Miss Jean curtains was open, checking his watch he realised that it was time for the show. Miss Jean was on time in showing the street her body. She ran her hands slowly over her, stopping for a short while to caress her frim-rounded breasts. Munroe kept his eyes firmly fixed on her. Just then, John-Smith came back into the room. Munroe turned his gaze from the window and walked over towards John-Smith. Handing over the crow bar Munroe started to prise the floorboards up. After lifting up three of the floorboards Munroe and John-Smith looked down into the dark space. Apart from the dust and cobwebs, a pool of blood had gathered between the floor struts. The lack of air had not turned it into a dry seen. The amount told both detectives that the professor had all most bled to death. What the torturer had done by stitching his stratum was to prolong his life for further endearment in pain leading to the slow death by hanging. Munroe still looking in the deaths of the floorboards wounded if the professor had reviled any secrets that he had. Ray noticed that John-Smith had started to prise up the other floorboards. Soon more boards had been removed. Again, apart from the dust and cobwebs John-Smith noticed a larger area of dampness that had spread. Munroe knelt down and ran his hand across the dampness. Lifting his hand towards his face, he saw that it was wet. To find out what it was they needed the help of the forensic people. Munroe left the room and headed down stairs to find the Wilson still sitting in the front room. Both wondering what the noise was. Mrs Wilson was doing her knitting while Mr Wilson was reading the paper. Mr Wilson dropped the paper onto his lap when Munroe entered. After phoning the station, Munroe sat across from the Wilson, how was he to tell them that they had to move out due to what they had uncovered. Best way was to come straight out with it. Mrs Wilson burst into tears not realising what Munroe had said. "Why now" said Mr Wilson. We have uncovered that the professor had been tortured before he was hanged. We are now treating your entire home as a murder seen. The more we uncover the more we can pitch together what happened. Munroe waited until the Wilson gathered their thoughts, in the meantime his eyes glanced up towards the ceiling. What he noticed was a large damp patch forming. Mr Wilson noticed Munroe stare. "It started when you first came. I took no notice of it due to the circumstances and what was going on at the time. Since then it has become Worst". "The room above I presume it's that of the late Professor". "It is". Is that where you have been lifting the floorboards? Enquired, Mr Wilson. Munroe had a long look at him before he answered. "Am sorry but at this moment I cannot revel what we have found, just to say that we will spending more time here from now on.

Mrs Wilson walked back in after phoning their daughter. She told her husband that they could travel as soon as they were ready. Just then, the forensic team arrived. Munroe excused himself and met the team at the front door. After a short brief, the forensic team made their way up stairs to carry out the long consuming search of both rooms.

14

Mr and Mrs Wilson quickly packed their suitcases and made their way outside, stopping briefly to have a last look at their home before stepping out though the front door, they met Miss Jean who had a quite word. Being nosey, she wanted to know how the case was going on. Sensing she had been observed, Miss Jean tilted her head to the upstairs bedroom. Munroe peering from the bedroom window saw what was going on and nodded his head... He turned to John-Smith who was watching the forensic team at work. "Any think yet" John-Smith walked over then told Ray that the dampness was caused by a larger amount of water. What type of water they cannot say until they get back to the lab? Munroe looking puzzled at what he had, been told. "Remember that witness report stating that the supposed professor was carrying a large package, which was heavy and damp". "What of it" said John-Smith? Suppose that this package was a large ice block. It would explain the amount of water and explain why it took the professor longer to hang than normal. Are you saying that after his torture hand taken place the professor had then been placed on the block of ice to make it look like he had been hanged a slow death? "That would explain the medical report concerning frostbite," said John-Smith. With both eardrums punched, he had no way of calling out even if he managed to spit out the wadding. The last sentence seemed to hang in mid-air for a while. Both detectives' minds considered the implication what they had both said and to visualise the amount of suffering Professor Churchill had gone though. The weather would have made the ice block melt more slowly tightening the rope around his neck in every inch the water melted away. Whoever had carried this grotesque ordeal out had no thought of what he was doing to another human being. It was if he had pleasure in doing it.

Munroe walked to the rear of the house into the kitchen. Finding the key to unlock the door he stepped outside. To his front, a small courtyard neatly kept clean, even if it was coved in snow. To his left was the outside toilet. What brought his attention was a ladder leaning on to the adjourning fence. Stepping on to the ladder he slowly looked over to MR Dolek garden. What he noticed were footprints, which had almost, been covered with the falling snow. Not bothering to turn around he asked John-Smith if Mr Dolek was wheel chair bound. John-Smith said that as far as he knew he could not walk. Stepping down Munroe entered the kitchen followed by John-Smith, they both walked to the front door. Munroe was about to turn the handle when John-Smith asked what he had seen. Ray told him that footprints over the fence lead to Mr Dolek back door. If you say that he cannot walk, who then made the prints. Asked Munroe.

Mr Dolek shouted to the detectives to come in. He was in his chair facing the window when the detectives entered the front room. "Did you see the floor show," said Mr Dolek to Munroe. Ray smiled then said he had. John-Smith looking puzzled would ask the question once he was alone with Munroe. John-smith left them alone and walked towards the rear of the house. In the kitchen, he noticed a cigarette ashtray sitting on the kitchen table. Inside amongst the squashed cigarette ends was the same sort of tip he had picked up from the RAF base. Sniffing the air, John-Smith could just make out the same smell of sent he had smelt while taking to Kessler. He had found what he was hopping for; his hunch had paid off... Kessler had been in this house.

Returning to the front room, he gave Munroe a nod. Munroe walked over so that they could talk in private without Dolek over hearing. John-Smith quickly told him what he had found. Munroe turned around and approached Mr Dolek. Without any hesitation, Munroe asked how he had known Heir Friedrich Kessler. Dolek sat slummed in his chair once he heard the name Kessler. His eyes fixed steering though the window his memory traveling back in time almost lost in what was going on around him. After a few minutes Dolek Cleared his throat, he began to tell his story.

As my name might suggest it is not English, it is Polish and I am a Jew. I was born in Krakow in Poland, in happier days than they are now. Both my parents left Poland when I was about three years old. My father was working for the Polish Government traveling back and forth to Germany, spending weeks apart from my Mother. When we came over here he started working in London, what he did he never mentioned it or told me even when I was older My Mother knew but it was her secrete. One day he told us that he was going away, that was the last time I saw him. My Mother told us that he would be away for some time, so my sister and I adjusted our lives without him. Even today, I still do not know what my father did, until Kessler turned up. He told me that my father had been arrested for spying and had been imprisoned. "How did Kessler find out where you lived?" asked Munroe. Dolek again stirred out though the window, his eyes started to fill up with tears. When he finally brought him, self to continue, his voice changed to sadness. Kessler had the delight in telling me that when they had finished interrogating him he told them all what they needed to know. They started by pulling his fingernails out slowly. After my Father still refused to talk, they then pulled his toenails out. Still after hours of pain he finally gave in when they smashed, each toe to a plump with a hammer “Where is your father now?” asked Munroe. Dolek moved his eyes from the window then looked at Munroe. Kessler said he was in a prison in Germany. Munroe looked hard at Dolek before he asked the next question. “What I cannot understand is why he made contact with you” Dolek said that due to the Professor lodging next door he wanted a safe house.” How did he know that the professor was there?” asked John-smith. A man with a slight limp came to my home weeks before Kessler turned up saying that my Father had been arrested and if I wanted to see him, again I was to do as I was told. He told me to take notes of the timings of this man next door. At the time, I had no idea who he was or what they wanted from him. It was not until Kessler turned up did I know what they were upon. “How” I overheard both of them talking in the kitchen, they were speaking in German, which I could understand. When was the last time you saw Kessler? Asked Munroe. It must have been round about the23rd or 24th I cannot be Shaw. In addition, the man with the limp when did you last see him? I cart be positive it might be the 23rd. I do know that he had blood splatted over his jacket and hands and he was smiling. He gave me a cold stare before he left, I have not seen him since. Could you give a description of this man with the limp? Dolek nodded his head. John-Smith final question was “where was his sister” Dolek turned sharply towards John – Smith his hand clasped together in a form of pray. “They have her “Munroe looked at John-Smith Dolek had been through it all he knew deep down that both his Father and Sister where dead. What will happen to me now? John-Smith said he would be arrested for adding and a betting in a murder case. Munroe started to walk towards the front door, stopped turned round then said “Why didn’t you come clean and tell the authorises of what was going on” Dolek one question answer was “would you” Munroe smiled turned the handle and stepped outside he was thinking of Karan. Over his shoulder he said, “No I would not” The door closed behind them leaving Dolek alone.

15

Karen watched Ray Munroe drive away in the cold crisp morning snow. She walked the short distance to the kitchen making Shaw the door had been locked before she went upstairs. Duke barked as Karen was about to leave the kitchen, she looked at him with hands on her slender waist. Turning the door key, again Karen slowly opened the door to let in the fresh cool wind enter the kitchen The cool wind soon wrapped itself around Karen exposed naked body; she quickly pulled her dressing robe around her shutting out the cool inviting air. Duke bounded though the door once he had finished he too was feeling the bitter wind. Karen slowly made her way up stairs to get dressed. Feeling fresh, she reached down the suitcase from the top of the wardrobe. Packing clothes, which she thought they would need. Karen carried the case down stairs placing it near the front door. Just then, the doorbell rang sending a loud echoing sound though out the house twisting her head around Karen noticed the silhouette of a man standing on the doorstep. With Duke by her side, Karan slowly opened the door. "Morning Karen" said the Brigadier. Karen smiled and opened the door. The Brigadier patted Duke on the head and walked into the front room. Karen followed. "Ray phoned from the office to ask if I would pick you up," said the Brigadier. Karan looked at him and wondered what else Ray had said to him, but decided not to aske. Karen excused herself and went into the hall to phone Mrs Churchill. The butler picked up the phone kept ringing finally it. Karen asked if she could speak to Mrs Churchill. She could hear words being spoken in the distance, words she could make out where "be careful in what you say" it sounded like the Butler was telling her to say or not. Mrs Churchill came on the line she sounded nerviest. Karen being careful in what she said asked her if she would care to spend a few days with them. A long pause followed before she gave her answer. Mrs Churchill sounding more cheerful said she be delighted. She would pack a few things and catch the midday train to Lincoln. Before Karen hung up, she told Mrs Churchill that she did not need to bring the Butler with them, Karen waited for a reply in a deep slow quite voice said, and "She would try". Karen replaced the phone then walked back towards the Brigadier sensing that all was not well in the Churchill residence.

Time passed slowly waiting for the clock to tell Karen it was time for them to drive down towards St Marks. On the way, Karen noticed the same man she had seen before who had whistled the tune. He was walking briskly towards them then suddenly stopped and turned the corner that lead the way to their house. Karen told the Brigadier to stop the car. He looked concerned then asked what was going on. Karen quickly told him what Ray and she had seen the other night. He quickly turned the car round and headed back. The man soon heard the car approaching turned round, stood, and stirred at the oncoming vehicle. He slowly pulled his hand from deep within his coat. Karen saw the revolver first and shouted to the Brigadier to stop; it was too late the well-aimed round shattered the windscreen sending fragments of glass in all directions. Karen let out a scheme of terror knowing the next round would find its mark. The Brigadier put his foot down and aimed the car straight at the man. Crack, crack went the sound of the revolver both bullets pissed the mark one round landed inches away sending a column of snow hurtling aimlessly away from them. The second Round imbedded it self-deep in the radiator. White columns of hot steam cascaded sky ward the Brigadiers field of view was limited. Karen felt the stunned impact sensing they had hit some thing or someone. The stranger was knocked to the kerb knocking the wind out of his toned body, by the time he had managed to stand the car had passed him sending a furry of snow witched covered him from head to toe. Brushing the snow away, the stranger noticed a pool of crimson blood against his left leg. The pain was numb to the touch. The stranger used his scarf as a makeshift bandage, and then watched the car disappear. A smile was on the strangers face with the wave of his hand he uttered the words "we shall meet again Mrs Munroe".

Round the first bend, the Brigadier found it hard to see where he was going. Karen leaned her head out of the passage window trying to direct him it was harder than she thought. Suddenly the White Heart came into view. Karan told the Brigadier to head for the rear of the pub. Harold Placeman was busy cleaning away the snow when Karen and the Brigadier entered the courtyard. Stunned by the appearance and the sound of the bullet-riddled car Harold though his broom to one side and made a dash to the hissing steaming car. Karen quickly opened her door; glass from the shattered windscreen fell onto the courtyard. The glass lay glistening in the morning sun only to be crushed by Harold to be buried deep into the already falling snow. Karen slowly stepped from the car a welcome hand guided her away from the hissing sound of the engine. Karen turned round to witness the Brigadier emerges from cloud of steam it was like watching a film in slow motion. Harold eyes gazed down at the already pool of blood forming at the feet of Karen. The bullet witched had shattered the windscreen had also caught Karen in the right shoulder. The wound was deep but luckily, for Karen the bullet had been deflected. Her injury was a four-inch gash to her upper shoulder. With the help from the Brigadier and Harold Karen slowly walked into the White Hart.

Karen slipped of her coat of her arm was covered in blood. The amount of blood made the wound look worse than it was. Harold fetched a bowl of warm water and bandage to dress the wound. Once the wound had been cleaned, it was made clear that Karen needed stitches. During all this time Harold had refrained from asking the question of what happened. He looked across at the Brigadier then at Karen who was placing her blood stained coat back on. "Is someone going to tell me what is going on?" said Harold. The Brigadier pulled Harold to one side. Karen watched as the he told him the story, glancing across at the kitchen clock Karen realised it was time to pick Mrs Churchill up. The Brigadier looked over the shoulder of Harold. He noticed that Karen was pointing to the clock. With a slight nod of his head, he told Harold that they soon had to be getting off. Harold turned around towards Karen after being told what had happened. Reaching inside his pocket Harold handed over the car keys to his car. Harold told the Brigadier that he would sort out his car, he knew someone who could soon fix it, in the mean time they could use his until there was fixed. Karen walked over and gently kissed Harold on the left cheek then headed out side.

Outside, Karen noticed the stained snow of blood now a reddish colour. Glaring across to her right arm she gently placed her left hand on the already throbbing pain remembering how lucky they had been. Karen heard the Brigadier snow-crunching footsteps approaching her quickly released her left arm to let it fall naturally on her left side. The Brigadier walked passed then turned looked hard at Karen before asking if she was okay. Karan gave a warm smile then walked the short distance towards the car.

The journey to the station went off we out any further incident. Karen checked her watch the London train would be arriving in less than five minutes. With the help from the brigadier, Karen entered the platform. The east wind made Karen shiver. Karan with the brigadier looked in the direction of the train that was approaching the station a long Colum of white steam covered the final approach making the train disappear only for it to enter the platform as by magic. A hiss from the engines breaks announced the train had come to a halt. White smoke lifted high into the morning sky blocking out the haze of the sun. Karen waited until Mrs Churchill stepped from the first class carriage. Karen noticed that she had helped the children down, making sure that they did not wander off. The Brigadier noticed that Karen was now holding her arm. He gave her a gently smile and reached out to support her in the sort distance towards meeting the Churchill's.

Mrs Churchill's eyes waded when she noticed that Karen was headed in her direction. Both embraced each other. Karen turned to the brigadier who she introduced to Mrs Churchill. "Pleasant trip" enquired the Brigadier. Mrs Churchill smiled and said that she and the children had had a most pleasant journey. With help from the station porter, the luggage was carried out to the waiting car.

The station platform was silent and empty when the last passage had disembarked. With the final whistle and the hiss from the breaks that sent a cloud of steam, a solitary click could be heard from the rear of the carriages. With the turn of the handle, a solitary man stepped on to the platform. He turned his coat collar up around his bear neck to shield it from the cold bitter wind. Reaching back inside the carriage the stranger retrieved a small suitcase then headed towards the station exit. He looked round when the train gathered speed watching until it disappeared down the winding track sending white smoke spiralling towards the waiting clouds.

16

Leaving Dolek, alone with in his own thoughts. DS Munroe with DC John-Smith Patten stopped on the snow-covered step closing the door behind them. John-Smith reached deep inside his pocket looking for his packet of Park Drive cigarettes. Handing one to Munroe they both inhaled deep letting the smoke drift away by the strong wind. "Where next" asked John-Smith. Munroe opened his door looked across the roof of the car then said "Wightman". Munroe took one glancing look at Dolek home then pulled the Ford slowly away. Leaving the street behind Munroe looking through his rear view mirror noticed the police car turn the corner it stopped outside Dolek's home. Two police officer's walked the few steps to his door. Before the final bend, Munroe witnessed Dolek being lead a way.

Traveling down Lindum Hill, passed the police station they soon reached Mr Wightman works. Munroe parked the Ford outside the main gates and walked the sort distance across the road to the lonely cold looking gate box. Munroe knocked sharply on the door. The door opened out wards Munroe having to step backwards before he was knocked down. A figure in uniform asked politely if he could help. Munroe slowly showed the guard his warrant card before asking to see Mr Wightman. The guard informed Munroe that Stan was on his break in the canteen. Pointing the way, without a further word the guard slammed the gate box door shut before Munroe could ask any more questions. Leaving Munroe and John-Smith standing alone. John-Smith turned his gaze to Munroe shrugged his shoulders then headed off towards the canteen, muttering to himself.

Stamping their feet to clear the snow off both detectives entered the canteen. A solitary figure sat near the stove in the far corner rubbing his hands together. Munroe opened his coat and walked over, before they were half way across Mr Wightman stood up with his back to both detectives. John-Smith called out his name, Mr Wightman turned around his face cringed as if he was expecting someone else. "I have been expecting you to turn up," said Mr Wightman. Munroe pulled over a chair and sat near the stove rubbing his hands together to get the circulation back before he stated to speak. Mr Wightman was dressed in his security uniform he looked the part. Munroe noticed a face that had weathered more storms than he could have hopped. He had a scar running from his left ear towards the corner of his mouth. Wightman noticed Munroe looking, he eased his left arm towards his face trying to conceal the scar only to realise that it was too late. His eyes were bright telling a tail that only he knew the answer too. Munroe also noticed that his hands where those of a man who was not freighted of work.

Munroe started by saying why he was expecting them. Mr Wightman looked from one detective to the other before sitting down facing them. "My daughter Jean said you had called round asking questions" Since then I have been waiting for your visit. John-Smith asked what

he could tell them about Professor Churchill. Wightman started by saying that they had first met in early November when he pulled up by taxi. He looked a solitary figure standing there. "Why" asked Munroe. He stood there for a long time deep in his own world, looking up and down the street. Then he suddenly turned around and waved as if he knew I was watching him, or if he was making sure, someone was not watching him. It felt strange and eerie. The next day I was leaving for work at the normal
Time when I heard a voice shouting at me. Stopping to see whom it was I was shocked to see
The professor running to catch me up. It turned out that he was going to be working at the same works. "Did he ever discus what type of work he was doing" Wightman stood up to Stretch his legs before he continued. No that matter never passed his lips. He mostly talked about his family in London. He did say a very strange commit one morning in December after he had been at the Wilson for a while. The professor told me that he thought he had been followed; he never mentioned it again, so I presumed that he must have been imagining it all. "Did you ever see or witness any stranger following the professor". Asked John-Smith. A movement of the head from side to side-gave John-Smith the answer. Munroe wonted too know on the occasions that he saw the professor, was he carrying a brief case. Wightman was silent for a long time before he answered. When he did, his commit startled both detectives. Wightman old them that the professor was

never without it. What stuck him as being odd was that before the works closed for Christmas the day before I saw him walking though the works gate without it, but noticed that he was carrying it when he left. Munroe reached into his jacket pocket retrieving his notebook. Flicking though the endless pages he finally came to the page he was looking for. Looking at Wightman Munroe asked him to describe the brief case in detail hopping he would leave out one vital peace of the puzzle. Wightman began with the colour, clasp and finally the handle that was worn to almost falling apart. It matched the detail in Munroe's notebook that he had been given by the professors' wife apart from his initial that was embroidered in gold. Munroe placed his notebook back in his jacket he let; his hand rest inside the pocket before he withdrew it. John-Smith broke the silence by asking if he could tell us any more about the professor before they looked at his office. Wightman scratched his head he knew he had a secret to tell about the professor now was the time. "Before we go I have something to tell you both" Munroe stood up looked out through the window watching the work witch was going on. He noticed two workers carrying a large girder into the far distance shed, before he turned around. Wightman sensed that the detective was ready. Before the works finished for Christmas, the professor called me into his office. He looked worried as if a man who had the world knocked out of himself. I had never seen him look like that before. He told me to sit down. After a pause, he picked up his briefcase that was hanging from behind the door. In his hand was a brown envelope. The professor looked hard at me without uttering a word. When he finally spoke, his voice was harsh and anxious as if time was against him. He told me to hand this to you; apparently, you too have already spoken. Munroe's face dropped. John-Smith stirred at his long-term friend. Munroe moved towards the window again, the air out side was cold his breath leaving a damp impression on the wooden window frame. When he turned around his face had changed Munroe was smiling? What so funny remarket Wightman? Munroe remember when he had spoken to the professor. I received a phone call before Christmas; all the caller said was "a brown envelope is waiting" I even wrote what he said down. Munroe for the second time reached inside his jacket pocket taking out the scrap piece of paper with the same words written down. Wightman walked towards Munroe with the envelope out scratched. Hesitation stopped Munroe opening it straight away. Inside in scrolling handwriting Munroe read the following line "**Erroneous a slip of parchment information with a movable barrier in concealment"**. It was signed by Professor Churchill. Ray handed it over to John-Smith. Munroe walked again to the window, his mind travelled back to the first time he had seen the professor and witnessed his brutal murder. Without turning around, he asked Wightman why he had not handed the envelop into the police before now. Wightman told him that the professor said the time would come to hand the envelop over when you turned up here, and not until. Munroe sensed Professor Churchill new he was going to die and that I would be involved.

What does that mean asked John-Smith? Munroe startled by the sudden question brought Ray back to earth. He moved his head from side to side, and then said, "The late professor has left us the location of the missing documents." How said John-Smith. Its location is within the clue he has left us; all we have to do is solve it. Moreover, I know just the person who can help, and then I hope it will tell us why the professor was murdered.

Wightman was standing by the security door waiting to show the detectives the professor's office; he looked like he was in a hurry. John-smith noticed that Wightman was walking to the main door, given Munroe, a slight nudge they then followed Wightman outside. The air out side was bitter cold all three-sent columns of cold breath swirling towards the evening sky. A short walk brought the detectives to a soled wooded door. Climbing the flight of stairs Wightman unlocked the professor's door. The room was dark and cold; it felt like no one had entered the office for a long time. Munroe turned to Wightman "how long has this office been closed" Wightman fumbled with the light switch before answering. "The professor would have closed it on the 23rd of last month" Since then no one has entered, the only key is this one and the one the professor had. Munroe had a good look at the office he noticed that the writing table of soled oak was by the window allowing more light to enter through the high window. Professor Churchill's umbrella was still standing in an empty waste bin near the door. His writing fountain pen lay across the used blotting paper. Spare reading spectacles all so lay where the late professor had left them. It was like looking at a museum. John-Smith started looking through the endless books and paper witch littered the office. Munroe walked to the edge of the oak desk a solitary photo frame with a slight coving of dust stood alone. Studding it closely he was looking at a family photo. Taken a long time before he came to Lincoln. Gently he placed it back where it belonged. John-Smith joined him at the desk; Munroe looked at him then at the photo.

Wightman made an excursed cough John-Smith looked over his shoulder. Wightman said he had to get back to the gate, Munroe without turning around said they would be asking more question in due course. Wightman nodded then walked out, closing the door behind him.

Munroe turned to John-Smith then said, "Well what do you make of this" lifting his arms to indicate the littered office. John-Smith smiled then answered, "It's like a tale from a novel only we can solve it". Just then, the phone on the oak desk started to ring. After the third ring, Munroe picked up the receiver. "Good after noon detective Munroe" who is this asked Munroe. "Never mind my name it's of no importance. Nevertheless, we do have a common purpose in our quest to find the final papers of our dear late friend. Before I go, how is your wife? I here she was involved in, 'let's call it a small incident this morning'. Please pass on my concern, as we shall meet again. The phone went dead. Munroe slammed down the receiver. John-Smith took a step towards Munroe. "What going on" asked John-Smith. Karen has been in some sort of incident.

Both detectives hurried through the office door. Outside, watching through the glass panels of the telephone box stood the caller. Exiting the telephone box, the caller made his way to the gate sentry leaving behind a pool of crimson blood.

17

The gentleman stranger with a smile on his face walked the sort distance to the platform exit. Handing his ticket over to the waiting station porter, who was pounding his feet trying to keep them warm. Before leaving the station, he stopped to admire the remains of the bombed out waiting room. The station porter glanced in his direction before he commented that it was the work of a fascist then walked away.

Outside the only car, waiting was his lift. Hans noticed the tall figure approaching the car. He recognised the stranger from that dark cold night of torcher, his name was never mentioned. Climbing into the passage side the stranger could not help but notice that the divers left leg was covered in dry blood. Hans Smut moved his hand towards the bandage leg the pain was bearable he would sort it out later. “Good journey down” asked Hans. The stranger turned his head smiled then said “Yes” and my name is Heir Wolf Zimmerman

As they drove away from the station Hans told him what had happened this morning. “Did they get a good look at you?” asked Zimmerman. The brigadier might have done and as for the woman she was too freighted to look, laughed Hans. Zimmerman gave Hans a starring look then smiled. What about Dolek? My informant told me that he had been arrested this morning what will happen to him I cannot say. Wolf Zimmerman sensed that Dolek had served his time it was time to end it. "Tell your informant to pay him a visit" Zimmerman reached into his coat pocket and handed over a small package to Hans. "Give these to your informant, they are for Dolek to take" How it happens is no concern of mine, but it will be done. Alternatively, heads will roll, do I make my self-clear said Zimmerman. Hans looked at the package he understood the meaning of what was, expected from him. Hans nodded his head he would pass the package on to night.

"What of the brief case" asked Hans? Heir Wolf Zimmerman stirred out through the window watching the grey clouds moving endlessly away. Without turning his gaze towards Hans, he told him that Heir Kessler plane had been lost over the English Channel. The authorities reported that it was an accident all crew and passengers were lost, alone with the brief case. A moment of silence filled the car until Hans asked the question that was burning in side him. So why are you here Heir Zimmerman? He turned his gaze from looking through the window, before he answered. Before I explain my self, what did you find in the Professors office? Hans gripped the steering wheel hard making his knuckles turn white. His left leg aching in each movement of the pedal. "I made the phone call as instructed Munroe answered. Five minutes later he Munroe along with John-Smith left. Gaining entry was easy the door was unlocked but I am sorry to say I found no evidence of any copy of his notes. Zimmerman took a deep breath before he spoke. When he did, it came as a shock to Hans, "never mind Munroe will lead us to it".

Hans finally pulled the car to the boarding house. Switching the engine off Hans sat there his mind travelled back to what this man had done. Hans never knew his name until today. What Zimmerman had done to Professor Churchill would never leave his concuss mind was it worth the pain and torture he had inflected. The journey had not ended yet; more blood would spill on the paths of Lincoln before Zimmerman found what he was looking for.

Zimmerman opened his passenger door. Leaning into the back seat to retrieve his bag he walked to the driver's side, tapped on the window. Hans's stirred through the closed window. Gripping the handle Hans slowly wined down his window, letting in a cool breeze. Zimmerman slowly bent forward he looked straight into Hans eyes when he spoke it sent a shiver running down his back. "Make sure your informant carry's out my request". Hans new better than to argue with him he had seen what he was capable of doing. Professor Churchill was not the first human being to fall to his kind of torture. Before Hans pulled Away, Zimmerman told him to pick him up the following morning early, as they had important work to do for the fatherland.

Hans pulled away after watching him enter the guesthouse; he had a smile on his face. Streets away from where Hans had dropped of Heir Zimmerman he found the house of his informant. Stopping a good distance, away as not to draw attention to himself, Hans stopped and switched the engine off. The only sound he could hear was the howling wind blowing against the car. The interior of the car soon turned cold. He was fed up of the frizzing cold weather. Winter was dragging on in a few days it would be February. Stepping outside, he was met by the cold bitter wind, quickly Hans turned up his collar of his coat. The wind biting hard into his damaged leg making the pain feel worse than it was. Hans entered through the rear courtyard door. The deep snow had-covered the footpath that had not been walked on; looking behind he noticed the footprints which he had just made also noticing one of the prints had a slight pool of crimson blood laying on top like jam on a cream cake. Hans looked down at his left leg it was starting to bleed again. Reaching the rear door Hans hesitated before knocking. He saw movement in the kitchen and heard music. He gave the door three knocks and waited. The door was open after a few seconds. Both stirred at each other before either one spoke. Hans smiled when he noticed that his informant was dressed in only a small night robe.

Hello Jean, it has been a while. Jean Wightman mouth dropped when she recognised who it was. The last time she had seen him was the very same day professor Churchill was found dead. Hans had been standing on the corner of the street watching and waiting. That was the last time Jean had seen him until now. Hans did not know that he had been spotted his plan was to watch then report back to London. Jean suspected that he had something to do with murder. The first time they had met was in Hospital. Hans had come in to have an old wound looked at. She, Jean was the sister on call. A few days after they were going on a date all was going fine for the months that followed. Until Hans dropped, the bombshell. Jean had a secret only she knew. He told her that he knew she was taking drugs from the drugs trolley for her on use. How he found out Hans never told her it was his secret but now was payback time. He told Jean that he wanted her to make friends with Professor Churchill and to record his movement. Jean asked why, it was a matter that she need not worry about. Since that encounter, Jean had passed on the information she could gather. She knew if she failed, her career in nursing would be over. She had no option but to carry on. Now standing on the doorstep her life was in his hands again, for what purpose she would soon find out.

Hans walked into the kitchen then sat down near the open fire. The heat warmed his damaged leg. Jean noticed the blood stained trouser leg. “What happened?” asked Jean. Hans told her that he had an accident with a glint in his eye. Why come here why not go to the hospital enquired Jean. Too many questions would be asked I need your help. Jean walked over to the stove placing the kettle on for hot water. Meanwhile Jean fetched her first aid box. Hans rolled up his trouser leg to reveal the damaged that the car had done. The leg was a mess. The car bumper had removed a lot of the skin opening it down to all most to the bone. It needs stitching said Jean. Hans smiled he knew that she could sort him out. It would hurt that he was sure off but it would worth the pain.

Jean pawed the streaming hot water into a bowl and placed it near the leg of the chair. Jean knelt down in front of Hans, her robe falling apart over her thighs. Hans noticed Jean had no pants on.

Jean sensed his piercing eyes were between her legs; it made her feel sexy. Slowly Jean adjusted her position to reveal her pubic hair, exposing her wet and Horney vulva. Jean gently, started to clean up the exposed wound, the hot water made Hans tighten his grip on the chair the pain he felt seemed to last forever was unbearable. Once the cleaning of the wound had finished the pain running through his body eased. Jean moved the now stained crimson cloth along with the colour water to one side, in doing so the robe opened more to show Hans the full ness of her breasts. Jeans nipples Harden to the air, which moved gently over them. Hans looked into Jeans green eyes he wanted her now, more now than he ever did. Jean realised she was turning him on, she too wonted to feel him deep inside her but that had to wait. After Jean had threaded the tinny needle, she held it towards Hans, the thread dangling in slow motion. He nodded he knew what was to come. Pain would be slow to clear. The needle pierced the open skin sending shock wave through Hans's body he could fell the skin being pulled together by each stich that Jean made after the fourth snitch Hans passed out. Jean continued and managed to close the wound together; her handy work had saved Hans from losing his leg. Later Hans woke on the settee how he got to the front room he could not remember. The pain in his leg had eased it felt stiff and swollen. Hans new he would find it hard to get about. He thought of Mr Lowe and what he would have to say. Hans closed his eyes, for a brief moment remembering the happy time he had spent with Jean. If only their life has had been different.

Jean walked in with a hot cup of sweet tea. Hans opened his eyes moved his body to sit up taking the cup in both hands. His eyes followed Jean everywhere she went. She walked over and stopped at the window sliding the curtains closed. When Jean turned around she slowly untied her robe letting it fall to the carpet. Hans watched the robe drifted slowly down wards like it was in slow motion. Jean stood there for a moment moving her hands over her body caressing her nipples pinching them to make the hard. Once she was satisfied, Jean moved her left hand between her thighs her fingers moving up and down her vulva. Hans watched we glee he wanted her more than ever. He stretched out his hand in a gesture for her to come. Jean moved towards him. She could see his swollen man hood lying hidden. Slowly Jean pulled down his trousers and eased herself on him. Jean could feel him slide deep and hard in side her. The thrust went on and on until she felt him reach the end of her deep and pleasurable part of her body. Jean moved her hips up and down slowly teasing Hans to almost to the point of letting his man hood slip out from her. Hans clasped Jean's tender breasts his fingers caressing the erect nipples, his mouth tenderly sucking each nipple in turn. Hans could feel him self- ready to explode with a final thrust he pushed himself deep inside Jean. Jean could feel his warm climax ooze from him, a moment later she could fell her self-climax, a longing pleasure she had not had for a long time. Jean tensed her body while still sitting on Hans. She lifted her arms towards the celling trying to push him deeper inside her. She wanted this to last. Finally, Jean moved and eased herself of Hans. She could still feel the stiffness of him inside while picking up her robe. Jean moved back to the closed curtains. Pulling them, apart Jean noticed that it had started to snow again. Turning around Jean noticed that Hans was standing up. He reached deep inside his pocket. Warped in a tiny cloth were two tablets. "What's that?" asked Jean as she came closer. Hans looked deep into Jeans eyes then down towards the tablets. "I won't you to take these to Dolek in prison to night" What are they Hans. He did not lie to her. Hans told her that they would end his life.

Jean started to cry. I cannot do this to a friend. If you do not, then you will end up in prison a long side him the chores are yours. Jeans mouth dropped she could not come to terms in what he was saying. She looked hard at Hans trying to find what had changed him into a monster he had become. They had been lovers now looking back she realised it had all been a front in gaining her trust so he could use their relationship in gain information to black mail her. Hans clasped his hands tightly around Jean he wanted to feel the warmth of Jean for the last time. His eyes looked like they were ready to cry, without any further words; Hans gave Jean a tender loving kiss on the right check then headed off towards the kitchen door. Standing on the kitchen step for the last time Hans adjusted his collar to fend off the swirling snowfall. Without turning around, he slowly closed the door and made his was to rear courtyard gate, he knew he would never see Jean again. Before he opened, the courtyard gate tears had started to flow down his cheeks, he stopped briefly with his hand resting on the handle. With his composure restored, the gate was open. With a final click of the lock, the gate was firmly closed behind him.

18

Ray Munroe slammed down the receiver after the phone call concerning Karen accident then headed straight to the Ford. Both detectives climbed in without uttering a word. Ray put his foot down hard on the accelerator trying to gain that extra bit of speed. The old Ford battled hard skedding and sliding on the new soft snow in the race to reach Karen. In the far of distance John-Smith, looking though the haze of the heavy snowfall saw the manor. The manor was standing proud amongst the snow-covered trees. Its tall battlement's reaching high in the late afternoon sky.

Ray brought the Ford to a sliding halt just missing the ornate statue of a figure. John Knight the faithful butler was waiting on the doorstep. His face taught with grief and anger. Munroe noticed two cars parked in the snow covered drive. One he knew belonged to the family doctor the other he was not so sure of. Hurrying up the concrete steps Munroe stopped before entering the manor. John Knight explained that Mrs Churchill was in the drawing room and Mistress Karen was in her room. Ray thanked him.

Munroe stood at the bottom of the oak staircases for a few moments, glazing up wards wondering what he would see when he opened the bedroom door. With two steps at a time, Ray was soon outside Karen's bedroom. He knocks once then entered. Karen was lying down supported by pillows. She looked round on hearing the knock, smiled when she saw it was Ray. Munroe made his way to the opposite side of the bed. He held his wife's hand his eyes firmly fixed on hers. The Doctor did a slight cough making saw he covered his mouth. Munroe taken his eyes from Karen glanced over the bed to the Doctor. The Doctor quickly explained Karan's wounds. Munroe noticed a coloured porcelain blow near the bed the water now red from Karen's wound. The family doctor when he had finished wiped his hands, rolled down his shirtsleeves and replaced his tweed jacket. He told Karen to rest for a few days smiling as he did so. Munroe reached over the bed and shook hands with Doctor Kent. He had been the family doctor since Munroe was a small boy; his age was against him these days but continued to support the Munroe family. Ray walked Doctor Kent to the bedroom door, both shook hands before the Doctor turned and slowly descended the oak staircase to be, greeted by the Brigadier. Munroe eased the door closed Karen eyes were shut he made saw that the bed covers were pulled up towards her neck then creeping quietly he made his way to the bedroom door. Standing on the other side of the door Munroe took a long deep breath of relief, that his wife was not seriously hurt. He could hear voices down stairs a moment pause before he joined them.

In the drawing room, Mrs Churchill seated alongside Elisabeth looked round when Munroe entered. John-Smith standing with the Brigadier looked round when Munroe moved across the bright colour carpet. He kissed Elisabeth tenderly on the side of the cheek, before shaking hands with Mrs Churchill. Elisabeth asked how Karen was Ray mentioned that she was sleep.

Munroe wonted to know what had happened to his wife, his father sensed his son yeaning. He excused himself from both ladies. John-Smith followed the father and son to the adoring room closing the sliding doors shut. The Brigadier explained the circumstances leading up to the shooting. Both detectives listened without any interruptions. After he had finished John-Smith asked if the attacker had been hurt. The Brigadier was positive that the front left had side of the car had struck him hard on the left leg. He noticed that he was still standing once they had turned the corner looking through the rear mirror. The Brigadier looked at his son then asked the question "who is this man" Munroe turned away before facing his father. "We believe him to be involved with the killing of the professor" and we believe this man had connecting with the bombing at the station. "So why is he trying to kill you and Karen?" John-Smith answered by staying that the late professor had been working on a devise well advanced for its time in detecting aircraft. The Germans new of this and sent an agent over to retrieve it at any cost. They succeeded in torturing the professor. Unknown to them what they had was a forgery. The really planes are still hidden; they know of this and will stop at nothing to get their hands on it." Do you know where these planes are" asked the Brigadier. Munroe smiled then said no but I know a person who does. The Brigadier looked puzzled but new better not to aske. Munroe left both men talking then entered the drawing room.

Elizabeth had taken her leave and gone up stairs to check on Karen. Mrs Churchill was patting Duke when Munroe walked over to the roaring open fire. He asked if she had had a good journey down from London. Mrs Churchill smiled and said that they all had a splined time. The children enjoyed it immensely. Munroe reached into his jacket pocket retrieving the note he had written down on Christmas Eve. Before he showed her the note, Munroe wonted to know what her butler was doing while she was away. Mrs Churchill informed Munroe that he had told her that he would be going game hunting. "Did he say where he was going?" asked Ray. Mrs Churchill smiled. Why are you smiling? Mrs Churchill said that she never thought that he was the type of person to kill any thing. "Did he leave when you did" No he said he would travel a few days later. He drove us to the station then went back to the house. "Are you saw he went back to the house" I presume he did I could not be certain that he did, as soon we arrived at the station a porter collected our baggage and escorted us to the waiting train. "Why" asked Mrs Churchill. No matter it is not important. Munroe would get John-Smith to check on who disembarked on the train the same time as Mrs Churchill.

Munroe looked at Mrs Churchill for a while her face glowing in the evening light. He thought how attractive she was. Before he could explain the note, Mrs Churchill glanced her eyes upon Munroe studying him closely then said, "Would you mind if you addressed me by my Christian name" Ray smiled and informed her that it would be an honour. Then please call me Mary. Munroe handed Mary the note. She studied it for a great length before saying that it as from her late husband. "How did you know it was from him" Mary said that they would often have a game of using words in making up a sentence. "When did you get the note?" asked Mary. Munroe told her that he had a phone call late on Christmas Eve; the caller did not revile his name. Nevertheless, he said they would meet one day unfortunately, that day did not happen. Mary looked hard into the glowing fire remembering the last time that her husband and she saw each other. It seemed such a long, long, time ago.

Munroe waited a while before asking if Mary new what the note said. Mary asked for a pencil and paper then started to write down the answer to the note. When she had finished Mary passed the paper to Ray. "**False Door Panel Document Behind**" Munroe smiled so it was still inside the professor's office. Mary asked was did it mean. Ray told her that the Original planes for the radar were in his office. So why was he killed if the planes are still there? Ray sat beside Mary and told her all what he knew, from the very start.

19

Jean Wightman waited in a light fall of snow until the heavy wooden gates to Lincoln prison opened. The prison built in 1872 replaced the old prison that was housed in the grounds of Lincoln Castle. Inside the place looked dark and era a place she hopped, she would not visit again. Her name was called forward by a tall prison warden. Both stood in silence the warden checked his notes of visitors causally taking his eyes form his board to have a good look at Jean. Satisfied that she was who she said she was Jean was ushered to the waiting room. Jean noticed that young children were playing in one corner of the room; they seemed to be oblivion in the surroundings and the meaning of what the prison stood for. In their world, they were happy playing together. Amongst the continued talking and shouting from the children, Jean sat in silence her eyes darting from group of mothers to another. Her thought of her past and present was interrupted by the sound of a heavy door being open. Two large looking wardens entered keys hanging lose from their waists swaying from side to side as they made their way to the centre of the room. The children stopped playing frighten in the appearance of these men. One hurriedly ran to his mother.
The warden read out a list of names, Jean was last. Following each other, the group entered the courtyard stepping on to the cobblestones. Each footstep made an echoing sound witch bounced from the tall prison walls. Gazing upwards Jean noticed that a few inmates where

peering down at the group, one man was making a rude jester with his hand.

Inside the stone building, the air smelt damp and cold. The warden escorted Jean to the adjuring room. Inside placed in the centre was a small table. Jean placed the wicker picket basket to one end of the table. Moving out the solitary chair Jean sat down and waited. Looking around the bear cold walls covered in white paint, her eyes noticed the high narrow window with rustic metal bars. The late afternoon sun was breaking through the bars casting a shadow on the far wall. Jean followed the light looking at the shadow. Suddenly the cell door opened Dolek was pushed in towards the table. Jean stood up and gently kissed his left cheek. Dolek placed his arm on hers and smiled. The warden informed Jean that she had thirty minutes, then turned and walked out. Jean heard the key being inserted into the wooden cell door. They had been locked in.

Jean removed the red and white coloured towel covering the basket. Placing the flask on the table first, Jean started to paw the hot steaming soup. The smell and steam drifted high to the celling. Jean had already smeared the lethal pill around the rim of the cup in which Dolek would drink. Taken the soup in both hands he started to drink. Jean noticed that he had lost weight in only a sort amount of time. He also carried a swollen right eye with heavy bruising around it. Jean plated up the remaining food. "How are you?" asked Jean. Dolek looked over the rim of the cup before speaking. Dolek told her that they are treating him okay. When he had first come here, he was made to strip. He sat in his chair for an hour with the window wide open before they came with these stripe clothing. Dolek pulled at his shirtsleeve. “And your eye” asked Jean. Dolek placed the cup down lifted his hand too his swollen eye remembering how it happened. He told Jean that once he been shown to his cell the other prisoners inside gathered around him. They started asking question about the murder of Professor Churchill. Equating him, he was a Polish spy. Spiting and prodding him. This kept on and on until one decided to hit me. When he had finished the others started. Dolek lifted his shirt up showing Jean the dark bruising which covered most of his body. He started to cry sobbing that he wanted all this to end. Jean placed her arms around him knowing that in a few minutes his wish would come true. Suddenly Dolek smiled his face turning more pale looked into Jeans eyes. It seemed to Jean he knew what she had done to ease his pain. Before the warden opened, the wooden door Dolek told her that he used to watch her parading around her room naked. Jean embarrassed in what he was saying felt turned on in the thought that she had given him pleasure in showing him her body.

The door to the cell opened with a bag. Time was up the thirty minutes brought to a sudden halt. Jean moved closer to Dolek to whisper in his ear. She kissed him on both cheeks, he held her hand for a brief moment, before the warden wheeled him though the open door. Dolek turned his head for one more glance at Jean. His eyes were dark and full of sadness but happy at the same time. Jean sat down with a heavy heart looking at the open door. Knowing that her lasting memory of Dolek would be him being, wheeled down the long corridor to his tiny cell. His end to life hanging on by a thread. The prison warden came back and told her it was time to go. Picking up her basket Jean had a long lasting look at the room. Moving her head to one side she looked up towards the bars the sun had gone dark clouds now covered the once blue sky.

Outside the prison gate, Jean adjusted her coat to the chill wind. She could feel the wind biting through her. Walking alone deep in what she had done to Dolek. Jean was unaware that a short distance behind her she was, being followed. In the still of the evening light, Jean heard the prison siren sounding; she knew that her friend Dolek had died.

Heir Wolf Zimmerman swung the P-38 up and, from point-blank range fired. The bullet caught Jean just below the left eye, exploding from the back of her head and tearing a whole the size of a tennis ball. She pitched backwards, a greyish slop of brain falling to the cobbles beneath her body. Thick blood bubbled through her long hair like water through reeds. Zimmerman fired again, the impact of the bullet twisting the body round, causing the lifeless arms to twitch as if they had still been animated. It was scarcely necessary to fire the third bullet. Or the fourth.

Zimmerman stood staring at the corpse for movement. He then wheeled around and walked away, from the lifeless body of Jean Wightman, picking up the picket basket at the same time.

Jeans body lay were she had fallen, crimson blood trickled along the cobblestones washing away the light snow turning the snow from white to a goulash red.

The warden who had escorted Jean through the prison gates found her an hour later.

20

Ray Munroe sat in silence when he had finished talking to Mary. She had not interrupted him once in the past hour. One of the questions that he had not for gotten to ask was about Mary's butler. Mary said that he had been with the family for about ten years, highly recommended, from whom Mary could not remember. "What is his name "asked Ray. Mr Lowe. "And where did you say he was going to" Mary cleared her throat and said, "He said he was going to Scotland game shooting at a place called Killen on the bank of Loch Jay. Slight teardrop slowly moved over her cheeks was the only movement Mary made. Listing intently in what Munroe was saying she found it hard to understand what he had uncovered about her late husband. She felt proud in the knowing she had been part of his life. What she wanted to know now was who had done this tradable inhuman act against him? Munroe walked over to the open fire. He was about to ask a question when the Brigadier entered followed by John-Smith. Crossing the long Arabian carpet John-Smith made his way to the French window. The sky had turned dark and cold, blustery wind started to howl amongst the trees. Just then, the phone in the hall rang. John Knight made his way to answer it. A knock on the drawing room door alerted the guest. The Butler entered cleared his throat then announced the call was for Ray Munroe. Ray made his excuse then followed John Knight into the hall. The phone lay dormant until he picked up the receiver. The caller told Munroe that there had been shooting not far from the prison and a body had been found. He also informed Ray that Dolek had been found slummed in his wheel chair dead in his cell. Munroe asked the constable to info DCI Cater they would meet him at the prison. Ray placed the receiver down and quickly told John-Smith what the caller had said. John-Smith month dropped when he heard that Dolek had been found dead. He had formed a likening to a man who had lost everything he once loved.

Ray was placing his coat on when Elisabeth came down the long stairs case. He looked up to her standing with her slender arm resting on the banister. "What's wrong" Ray moved closer to his mother he wanted to know how Karen was. "She still asleep" answered Elisabeth. Munroe told her that he had to go. He had been informed of a shooting taking place and a body had been found. She was worried that there might have been a connection with the Brigadier and Karen in counter. Munroe placed his hand on his mother's a reassurance in his eyes told her that it would be all right. John Knight was standing by the door. Munroe whispered something to him Elisabeth not quite knowing what was said looked at Munroe before the door was closed.

Outside in the dark cold of the night, John-Smith lit a cigarette handed one to Ray then proceeded to open the passenger door. Once inside the car the air was cold without the engine running. Ray Munroe selected first gear drove round the water feature and with a burst of acceleration headed towards the prison.

The sort journey to the prison was driven in silence. Once outside the prison warden met them. Both detectives stood talking and where just about to enter when DIC Carter drove up. Carter approached Munroe his hands thrust deep in his pockets, for warmth. With his head, he indicated to Munroe to move away from the other two. Ray followed. DCI Carter did not waste any time in what he said to Ray. Carter received a phone call from

London Chief Constable Martin informing him that they were interested in the shooting all information had to be treated as top secret. He did not give a reason he said you would understand. DCI Carter waited for a response. Munroe before he gave an answer to his DCI noticed in the far distance under a solitude street lamp, the light cased a dark shadow over

The lifeless body covered by a solitude blanket. One of the prison guards was standing hands deep in pockets guarding the corps.

Munroe remembering what had been said to him in London told his DCI what he needed to hear. The facts about the case what Munroe new would come later? Satisfied Cater walked with Munroe to the body. The prison warden who had reported the finding had returned to stay with body. Munroe searched his pockets for a cigarette he needed one before the blanket was removed. Sensing the police officer was looking for a cigarette the warden handed his open packet to Munroe. Pulling one out he placed it between his lips fumble with the lighter before the end of the cigarette glowed red. He exhaled deeply blowing out a long Colum of smoke. The smoke lingered before it started to diff up wards. Munroe gave the nod at the same time the warden knelt down and removed the damp stained blanket. What they both witnessed was a body, of a woman who shot at close range. Part of the face had been blown away the rest of the body could still be identified as a woman. DCI Carter knelt down beside the body he noticed the second shot had entered her chest. Munroe still smoking the last of the cigarette looked away. He knew who the dead person was. Carter stood up looked at Munroe. “You know who she is don’t you?” Munroe glanced down at her before saying that it was Jean Wightman. “What was she doing here?” asked Munroe. The warded told both of them that she had visited a pensioner named Dolek. “The same Dolek who was found dead in his cell” remarked Carter. Munroe just answered “Yes”. Munroe walked around the body stopping to look at the crimson blood. Following the discretion of the flow of liquid, he found what he was looking for the empty cartridge. Placing his pencil inside the cartridge, he removed it from the seen. The second cartridge witch had been fired at her chest would be found soon. Munroe remembered what he had said to Jean that he would find the saltant, who had murdered the professor now he would go to all lengths to find hers.

Two men dressed in white jackets approached the body carrying a stretcher to remove Jean Wightman. Gently lifting the body Munroe noticed part of Jeans organs laying beneath her. The men placed Jean on the stretcher moving her arms across her body before coving her with the blanket. Jean's last sight of daylight had, been covered forever. Munroe watched her been carried to the waiting vehicle. The rear doors closed with a clink making the sound seem louder in the quite ness of the evening. He watched the vehicle go before heading back to the prison. The detectives stood a short distance away and watched as the forensic team carried out a fingertip search of the seen. DCI Carter touched Munroe's arm turned then asked, "Do you think it's the same person who carried out both murders" Ray said nothing for a while then said he was sure that both murders were carried out by two different people. Moreover, Ray added that they were in some ways connected if not working together in finding the missing planes. DCI Carter looked up to the sky then said "What a bloody mess".

Munroe found John-Smith in Dolek's cell. He looked round the tiny room. One bed and a metal bucket was all the furniture Dolek had in his cell. Ray noticed a small pool of liquid on the floor beneath his wheel chair. The smell started to linger of urine.

John-Smith stepped outside the lingering smell of the cell followed by Munroe. "Well" asked Munroe. John-Smith scanned through the pages of his notebook until he found the right page. John-Smith told Munroe that

Jean Wrightman1 had visited Dolek this afternoon for about half an hour. The warden mentioned that she had brought a picket basket with her, nothing out of the ordinary. They were left alone in the visiting cell. The warden could hear talking and laughing, apart from that the visit was normal as it could be. "Did you say picket basket". Asked Ray. "Yes" The prison logbook entry mentioned that it contained a flask, sandwiches napkins and chicken protons. John-Smith stopped talking and looked at Munroe something was wrong in the way Ray Munroe was moving about. "What's wrong Ray?" asked John-Smith". Munroe stopped moving then said that there was no basket at Jean Wightmans body. "Did Dolek say anything on his way back to the cell?" asked Munroe. Only commit he made to the prison officer was to say that "she" looked better naked. Munroe smiled for the first time in a long while, remembering the show he had seen at her bedroom window. "How long did it take for the wardens to find him" John-Smith checked his notes again. They returned thirty minutes later. Munroe stepped back into the cell. Looking around he noticed a small metal cup lying under the bed. Picking the cup up Munroe noticed that it had been used. Smelling the rim of the cup Ray could smell that it had contained soup. Turning around to speak to the prison guard holding the cup high. Ray asked if Dolek had carried it back to his cell. The prison guard stayed silent for a while before answering. He gave a nod only then said Dolek had asked him if it would be all right. The prison guard said he could not see any harm in it.

Munroe only said that it might have killed him. "How" said John-Smith, the flask could not have contained poison as both had been seen drinking from the same flask. The prison warden stepped forward, by saying that they had gone back in the visiting cell and had noticed that Dolek and Miss Wightman were drinking at the same time. Munroe studied the metal cup by turning the cup over he noticed a very small mark with the letter "D" placed in the centre. A smile crept on Munroe's face. What so funny asked the prison warden? Munroe looked at both of them before telling them that Miss Wightman had smeared the rim of the cup with poison hence the make at the bottom of the cup. Jean wanted to be sure that Dolek cup was the right one. Nevertheless, why kill him. Ray walked back into the cell turned around then said he knew who had killed the Professor. However, that does not explain why Miss Wightman killed him remarked John-Smith. Munroe could only come up with the solution that whoever had made her do this, had a very deadly and sinister hold over her. The question was what.

Munroe walked away from the cold cell followed by John-Smith. Outside in the prison yard Munroe stopped and looked up to the top of the prison. The lights to the tiny cells in the evening light casted shadows on the cobblestones. The only sound to hear was the inmates talking of the death of the murderer who had killed the professor. Ray heard one saying it was justice paid in full. The tall wooden gate to Lincoln prison open to let the undertaker drive in, both watched the vehicle pull up to the rear were they kept the bodies of the dead. Munroe edge forward he had seen what he wanted to see. His next visit to this prison would be to make sure the killers where be hide bars. “Where now” asked John-Smith. Ray looked over his shoulder before answering. Munroe climbed into the ford started the engine, and then glanced over to John-smith before stating that they would pay a visit to the hospital. To find out what Nurse Wrightman was really like.

21

Lincoln Hospital stood proud in the evening light almost as it was telling the detectives that what lay beyond the wooded doors laid a dark and hidden secret. Both detectives approached the main reception. Two elderly people stood asking question before moving on. Munroe watched them head off down the long endless corridor. Ray turned around facing the middle edge woman be hide the desk. Munroe retrieved his warrant card showing the woman that they were the police. Startled by the present of the law the woman kept her voice down so as not to be, overheard by praying patents and staff who were milling about. "How can I help you?" Ray told her that they wanted to speck to the charge nurse on the ward that Nurse Jean Wrightman worked on. The woman flicked through the pages until she came across Jean name. Looking up she told them it was Ward B. John-Smith leaned over the desk and slightly asked what was on Ward B. With a deep sigh, she informed them that the ward was for those who were in intensive care. John-Smith thanked her and then headed off to find ward B. Climbing endless stairs both detectives reached the ward.

Munroe tried the door it was, closed. A notice in red bold words informed visitors to ring the bell. Ray kept his finger firmly pressed until a solitary nurse walked slowly to the waiting detectives. Pushing the door outwards the nurse with look of anguished asked what they wanted. John-Smith showed the nurse the warrant card. Stepping aside the detectives entered. Both noticed the quietness of the ward. Not a sound could, be heard in any of the rooms or down the corridor. The nurse knocked on the matron's door. The force of authority answered. Entering Munroe noticed that the matron was of middle age, a small woman with a concerning face. Different from the why she had addressed the nurse. "Gentlemen please take a seat" Removing their hats Munroe and John-Smith sat in front of the oblong desk. "How can I help you?" asked matron. Ray began by saying they were investigating the death of Jean Wightman. Slumber stillness filled the room before matron asked the question how. John-Smith told her Jean had, been shot. Quickly Ray followed on with the questions. How long has Jean be on the ward? Roughly about, six months. Jean had asked to be, transferred from the general ward. Why? Asked John-Smith. Matron stood up and opened the filling cabinet. Finally pulling out the file on Jean Wightman. Turning page after page matron came across the page she was looking for. Here it is, handing over the file to Munroe. Munroe read the file taking notes. Ray looked up at one point. "It says here that Jean had treated a patient with a leg wound." Matron said that the patient had been involved in accident. Jean mentioned him quite a lot when she was working. "In what way" asked Ray? Matron with smile told him that they had been going out together, and then all of a sudden the relationship ended. "Did this relationship in any away effect Jean's work" No on the contrary Jean's work has always been of the highest standard. The patients here on the ward talk of her with kindness and compassion. "I cannot understand why someone would won't to kill her" Munroe placed down the file then looked across the table before he finally informed the matron that they are looking into the possibility that she was being black mailed. "Why "asked the Matron. John-Smith thought of how to put the next question without trashing Jean reputation. Was Jean with her being on both wards able to take drugs away from the hospital without anyone noticing? Matron face dropped. I am afraid to say that it has happened in the past, but Jean was not that type of nurse I can assure you of that, remarked Matron. Munroe asked if Jean handed out drugs to the patient while on duty. Yes, she was one of our senor nurses and being so was authorised to hold the key to the drugs trolley. "How certain are you Matron that your patients did receive the drugs" asked Munroe. Further, more Matron Can you tell us what type of drugs are, used here on your ward? Matron sat back in her chair hands resting on her lap. She looked tried and she knew that by telling the detectives what they wanted to know would put the Hospital and Jean in the spot light. Further invitation by the hospital of the amount of drugs missing, answers had to be, found. "The most common drug we use here is "morphine". It eases the pain and in the end the patient's drift off without suffering. "Could this drug be addictive to someone who injects themselves? Enquired Ray. Yes, they can be hooked on it. What said effects would they have. Asked John-Smith. It depends on the individual. By taking this drug, the individual would use it for pain, too much and it would kill you. Stated Matron. Therefore, if Jean were taking the drug she would be using it for a reason. Most probable answered Matron. One final question Matron, the patient who came in with the leg wound would you have his name. Matron flipped through the file once more MR Hans Smut said Matron. Munroe smiled. Thank you. John-Smith almost knocking over the nurse who had let them in opened matron door. She quickly regained her balance and hurried down the corridor towards the ward. John-Smith smiled the word around the ward about Jean would soon be spread. Munroe was the last to leave; before he did, Matron touched his arm. He froze turned around and noticed tears forming in Matron Eyes. Ray new the question even though the lips on Matrons did not move. Ray whispered in her ear that he would let her know what the pathologists find out concerning Jean Wightman.

Reaching the parked Ford Munroe rested his hands on top of the Fords roof. John-Smith looked over from the opposite side. "What's next?" asked John-Smith. Ray glanced to the floor that Matron was working on before he answered. "We will wait until tomorrow, by then the pathologist report on both victims' should be ready. Both detectives drove away in silence.

22

Zimmerman lowered his pistol after he had fried the last round into the body of Jean. Smoke from the barrel drifted high over the lifeless body. Blood from the head wound streamed through her long hair along with parts of Jeans brain. Jeans body feel backwards in slow motion after the first round had entered her head bouncing once then settling as she hit the pavement. The remaining rounds fired at close range made her body switch even more. Lowe took one glancing look at the killing he had done. By now, the crimson blood had mixed with the snow turning it a pinkish colour. Slowly Zimmerman bent down, picked up Jeans picket basket, and walked off.

Hans sitting in the parked car a good distance away heard the first shot followed by four more. Where Hans had parked, he was unable to witness the brutal killing and who had been the target. Throwing his butt end out of the window Hans noticed Lowe walking towards him. Looking through the rear view mirror Hans could see that he was carrying a bag of some sort. Before Zimmerman reached the car, he hurled the basket high amongst the tall dark branches. The basket rested nicely from view. Heir Zimmerman smiled not even Detective Munroe would dream looking high amongst the tree.

Hans started the engine when Zimmerman opened the car door. Without saying a word, Hans drove away from the seen. Wolf Zimmerman turned his head to study him. His eyes firmly fixed to the road ahead. When Wolf started to talk Hans could tell by his voice that he had no remorse of what he had just carried out. What startled Hans more was the question he asked. "Where do Munroe's parents live? Hans took his eyes of the road for a brief second to look at Heir Wolf. Then asked "Why". Zimmerman adjusted his posture he felt incomputable in the way he was seating then he replayed. "They have a friend saying with them, I would love to meet." Hans slowed down at the next junction then headed off in the direction of the manor. Traveling up Bunkers Hill Hans passed a Ford traveling at speed. Mr Lowe glanced over his shoulder at the passing car, he noticed the driver. A smile formed on his face, turning around he settled down to the drive ahead.

Munroe's manor lay nettled amongst tall dark oak trees. Hans parked the car once Low told him to do so. Hans parked the car deep inside the wooded area away from other passing vehicles. Hans switched the engine of; silence filled the car the only sound coming from the trees. Lowe was the first one out. Hans lit a cigarette then slowly stepped outside the car. Both made their way through the snow-covered trees. Trudging through the deep snow made Hans leg ach. Mr Lowe stopped until Hans cached him up. "Problem with the leg" asked Lowe. Hans stopped and gently touched his leg the pain was getting worst. Hans said he would be okay. Without any further halts, both men approached the manor. They stopped short of the tree line. In front lay an open field, from there to the manor was a distance of five hundred yards. Mr Lowe calculated that the distance was too great to approach during day light; they would have to return when the time was right. Lowe unclipped the hasp on his binoculars case. Cleaning the lens Lowe started to view the Manor. Just then, the distance sound of a dog barking made both men stand still. It was not until Hans noticed that the dog had emerged from the side gate followed by the brigadier carrying a shotgun. Lowe raised the binoculars and trained them on the brigadier. He noticed that he was telling the dog to go and search were they were standing. Lowe slowly reached inside his coat to retrieve the pistol. His arm was steady feet slightly apart ready for the recoil. Hans observed the tension in Lowe face; he could feel and sense the moment. Duke stopped short of the tree line barking wildly looking straight at Hans and Lowe. Suddenly out of know where a hair darted between them leaping across the open vast space. Duke turned his head to follow the hair, one more look at the strangers then he too was off. Lowe lowered his pistol to his side. He raised his binoculars to see what the brigadier was doing. He could see him shouting at the dog, the wind making it hard to understand what he was shouting, about. Duke by now had lost sight of the hair, stopping to gain his breath he sat and starred. Finally, he caught the sound of the command standing up Duke made his way back towards the manor. Lowe kept his eye on them until both disappeared through the courtyard gate. He travelled his binoculars up to the first floor window. A solitude light flickered on. The curtains where still open; standing looking through the window stood Mary Churchill. The sight Lowe witnessed would remain with him for some time to come. Mary was standing with nothing on to cover her exposed breast. Ever since he had joined the Churchill's household, he had never seen Mary in the sight he was seeing now. Mary would have noticed the tiny footprints of the hair darting from one side of the snow-covered lawn to the other followed by Duke who was trying to catch it. Lowe kept his eyes firmly fixed on Mary his smirking face told it all leaking his dry lips in the pleasure he was seeing. He could only imagine what she would look like naked. Mary suddenly clasped her hands around her; someone else had entered the room. She moved away from sight of the prevailing Mr Lowe. The show had ended.

Hans stamped his feet he was feeling the bitter cold creeping through his shoes. Lowe replaced his binoculars back into the carrying case, turned and looked at Hans who was now rubbing his leg. "Did you get that fixed?" asked Lowe pointing to the leg. Hans stopped what he was doing, remembering what he and Jean had done only a few hours ago. His replay was a simple "Yes". "Was she good" What do you mean enquired Hans. "The nurse that stitched you up" "How did you know she was a nurse" "I know all about your nurse, I also know you had sex with her just this afternoon. Hans's mouth dropped like a stone. With a puzzled look, Hans asked "How". Simply you have just told me laughed Lowe, who turned and started to walk back towards the car laughing as he did so. Hans expression changed his Lawtey to this man was fading fast he could not wait to be rid of him finally. His time would come sooner than he had expected. Back in the car, Mr Lowe sat while Hans fumble for the key. Lowe looking straight ahead informed Hans that he knew every hoarded detail about him. It was his business to know. Hans started the engine without uttering a signal word. Hour later Hans had dropped Mr Lowe at his lodgings. Lowe walked around to Hans's side of the car, tapped on the window and waited until Hans had widened down the window. Lowe leaning his head close to Hans informed him that he needed to be, picked up at ten o'clock. Hans nodded then drove off to Yarbrough Road.

23

Mary Churchill climbed the carved scrolling staircase leading to her bedroom. Opening the door Marys eye caught sight of the four-poster bed, covered in a reach cream rose petal bed cover. Her dressing table had the same colour roses neatly arranged in an ornate vase standing to one side. The strong smell of reach perfume lingered throughout the room. Mary noticed that the washing bowl and jug had the same ornate design as the vase.

Putting aside her shoulder shawl Mary untied the leather strap securing her suitcase. Placing her evening dress neatly upon the bed. Mary slipped out of her traveling garments, she felt refreshed from the heavy woven dress she had been traveling in. Slowly Mary slipped out of her dress leaving on her petticoat. Standing in front of the mirror, she gazed at her slender figure she was proud of the way she looked after having two children. Mary started to undue her cream blouse buttons, once she had undone the last one she let the garment fall open. Her breasts pecking though the open blouse. Mary raised her left hand letting it run down her exposed cleavage feeling the tender feel of her soft skin. Her hand drop by her side when Mary slipped the blouse from her shoulders, the blouse dropped between her feet. Suddenly Mary heard Duke barking form outside her window. Slowly she walked the few paces across the rich carpet and stirred outside. Mary noticed Duke bounding across the open cover field after a hair. Mary thought what a delightful sight it was looking out amongst the tall trees covered in snow. Small patches of grass perturbing from the depths of the snow. Different from the concrete jungle of London, here she felt freedom for herself and her children. Mary stayed by the window unaware that from a distance she was been watched. She was capsulated by Duke and the hair; suddenly she heard the distance sound of the brigadier shouting. Mary watched as both man and dog disappeared through the courtyard gate.

Marys mind was far away dreaming of the happy times she had spent as a family and with her late husband. Still in a dream, Mary did not hear the bedroom door being open. She felt a slight coolness of cold running down her back, turning around she saw Elizabeth standing looking at her. Clasping her hands around her chest Mary reached for her blouse still lying where she had let it fall. "Sorry" said Elizabeth. I was in with Karan and heard you come into you room I wanted to make saw you were settled in all right. I did not mean to intrude. Mary smiled making saw the blouse was firmly around her. No other woman had seen her the way she was standing now; she did not feel it strange she felt liberated. Breaking the stale mate between them Mary commentated that she had heard Duke barking. Elizabeth crossed the sort distance between them and closed the curtains, turned around and said, "That the brigade went outside as Duke was uneasy to the extent that he thought someone might be outside". Mary looked beyond Elizabeth imaging that someone had seen her standing at the window with nothing on to cover her exposed breast; it sent a cold shiver down her bear back. Before Elizabeth left Mary, she told her that dinner would be at seven.

Mary walked over to the closed curtains after Elizabeth had gone. She slightly opened them to peer outside making saw in her own mind that no one was there. The two men who had been watching had long gone.

24

Munroe put the ford in gear to drive the short distance to John-Smith home from the hospital. John-Smith stepped on to the footpath the light was fading fast dark clouds loomed over head. He turned round to look at Ray who was staring straight ahead. “What’s wrong Ray?” asked John-Smith. Munroe had driven in silence all the way something was on his mind; he wanted to find out what it was. Munroe smiled before answering. Munroe informed him that he was going back to the station to find out the address of Hans, he wanted to find out what this man was really like. The only way he could do this was to ask the person beyond Jean Wightman and that was the neighbour. John-Smith looked at Ray then closed the door; he knew his partner had taken the murder of Jean hard. The only way he could come to terms with this was to find the answers by himself.

Entering the station Munroe approached the duty sergeant. Both looked at each other before Munroe asked him for the address of Hans. While Ray was waiting, DCI Carter slowly descended the stairs reading a police file. It was not until he was near the door did he notice Munroe standing talking to the sergeant. Walking over both men stepped to one side away from the counter. “Any further development” asked Carter. Munroe informed his DCI that they had just come from the hospital talked to the Matron. Anything of interest?

Only that nurse Wightman had transferred from the general ward to the intensive care ward six months ago. Do we know why? Enquired Carter. The Matron mentioned that after Wightman had treated this man while on the general ward did she apply for a transfer. Got a name. Munroe looked over the shoulder of the DCI the duty sergeant was waving a slip of paper, returning his attention to the question Ray told the DCI that the only name that came up was Hans Smut. Munroe moved away and approached the sergeant. Checking the name and address, he turned and walked back to Carter. Munroe handed the paper over to carter, interesting reading remarked carter. What is the next step? Remarked Carter. Ray folded the paper into his coat and walked the sort distance to the door turned then said "visit his neighbour.

The address witch Munroe was driving to was, number 7 Yarbrough Road it took less than ten minutes to get there. Parking a good distance away Munroe sat and watched noticing no movement he made his way across the wet and sluggish road. The neigh bough slowly moving the down stairs curtain witnessed his approach. Number seven curtains down and upstairs were still open.

Munroe stepped on the threshold of number six and knocked. An elderly man with a stick opened the door. "Can I help" Munroe reached for his warrant bandage. The old man stepped back stocked in seeing the police standing on his doorstep. Munroe smiled and told the old man that it was his neighbour that he was interested in. The old man moved to one side allowing Ray to enter. Munroe was, shown to the front room. Open fire greeted Ray the warmth soon warmed his cold hands. Both men sat aside the fire, the old man was first to speak. “Well what he done this time” pointing to the house next door said the old man. Munroe smiled. Nothing its some background information regarding Mr Smut I am interested in. “Oh I see, then fire away detective” Ray started by asking how long he had been next door. The old man said he had been here a good eight or ten year.

Lives on his own no trouble keeps himself to himself. Always speaks when he sees me, ask how I am and the like. Ray asked if he knew where he came from. The old man smiled showing Ray that most of his teeth were missing. “What so funny” asked Munroe. “You call yourself a detective asking a stupid question like that. “Like what” “Well asking where he came from with a name like Smut. He came over from Germany when both his parents had, been died when he was young. He said a leading party member had brought him up. “Did he say what member” Something to do with the security side. “What kind of work does he do?” asked Munroe. The old man said that he was a builder. He had a bad accident a few months back; hurt his left leg bad. Had to stop in hospital for a while. I did visit him once with a load of mail, postmark from Germany I noticed. When he came out he walked with a limp, it changed him he was more a recluse than he was before the accident. “What about friends” Never saw any, tell a lie I did see a young lass in his car once parked outside. Never saw her again. "Any male friend come calling" Again I never seen any. I have noticed that he has been using his car a lot these last few weeks, always coming back late at night. He thinks am a sleep but am not. I hear him creeping down the passageway trying not making a sound. One night I was tossing and turning so decided to make myself a drink. I heard his car pull up so switched the light off and watched. The snow was falling heavy but I could see that his clothes were wet, not from the snow. He came back out a few minutes later in fresh cloths then drove off again. I fell asleep so did not here in come back. "What month was this" It would be late December time I would say. "Any other strange happing's you can remember," The old man smiled again then said "he told me he was a spy" When he first came here I met him the local pub. He had had a few to many; he came over and sat down close like. He kept looking around before he told me "he had been sent over to spy for Germany". I just nodded. "Did you believe him?" asked Munroe. The old man shook his head from side to side. As I said, it was the beer talking nothing more. Munroe got up it was time to go. Before the old man opened his door, Munroe asked him not to mention our conversation to Mr Smut. The old man looked puzzled but new better than to ask. He told Ray that he would not, and by the way, my name is Gary-Gary Kent. Munroe nodded and smiled.

Ray Munroe crossed the road to his car. Lighting a cigarette, he waited until the tip turned red sending out a long Colum of smoke swilling around the ford before the smoke found a small opening to drift out through to the night air. Munroe started the engine; it was time to head back towards the manor.

25

Munroe gathered his thoughts while he drove back to the manor. He was certain that Smut was involved in the abduction of the professor and of the building that took place at the Wilson's home. What part he played if any in the murder and torture he still could not put that piece of the puzzle together. He still did not understand the connection to Jean or why he got involved with her. Hopefully by the time the autopsy has finished with her he would have more of the answers, for now Ray would have to wait. Driving home Munroe's mind was elsewhere, if he had concentrated he would have noticed the other car approaching at speed towards him. Only when it pasted was Munroe aware of the passing vehicle. Ray looked through the rear view mirror making a mental note of the number plate.

Ray soon pulled of the main road leading to the manor. The long track through the trees seemed to take forever. Half way down the snow-covered track Munroe had a sharp turn to the left, slowing down Munroe eased the ford round making Shaw he kept to the centre. Pulling out from the bend Munroe noticed a set of tier marks heading into the deep under growth of the trees. Ray stopped the ford looked at the tier marks, then in the general direction of the manor. He realised that by doing so a person could walk the distance under cover to the manor. His thoughts travailed back to the passing car putting a wave of IF'S. Munroe stopped the care and walked along the track marks. The marks soon came to a halt; Ray noticed that foliage had been placed to one side allowing the car to reverse back on to the track. Ray looked around until he found the fading footprints. Slowly he followed them until he reached the clearing. Standing under the cover of the trees Munroe could clearly see the manor standing alone and tenable to any person who might inflict harm to it. Looking around he noticed a small amount of fallen branches gathered together. Clearly, they had been stood on to fight off the cold dampness of the snow. Bending down Ray could see droplet of blood amongst the branches, he guessed that Hans Smut had been here along with another person with the amount of footprints left on the crisp snow. Whomever they were Munroe now realised they knew where he and Karan along with the rest of the family lived. The second man was cunning to say the least and very clever.

Munroe turned around and followed his own footprints back to his car. Tiny drops of rain stated to fall amongst the snow-covered branches, glancing up Ray noticed dark clouds forming; winter was almost to an end.

Ray drove the short distance towards the manor; raindrops pattered the tiny windscreen. Munroe pulled the ford to a stop the tyres' making a crouching sound amongst the gravel. The evening light was fading fast, heavy rain started to fall before Ray reached the main door. Before he had chance to turn the handle John Knight the butler opened the door. Duke bounded up to his master happy to see him. Both man and animal embraced. Entering the main dining room, the brigadier eased his chair away from the table and walked over to welcome Ray. Munroe noticed Karen was seating near the open fire, her left arm placed in a sling. Her eyes brighten when she saw her husband enter the room. Ray tenderly kissed her forehead squeezing her other hand as he did so. They could talk later in the privacy of the own bedroom.

Mary Churchill smiled in seeing the affection between them. Her own thoughts darting back to the happy time that she and her late husband had. Ray Munroe gently placed his hand on Marys shoulder, she acknowledges the jester of the touch. John Knight laid an extra space on the table, next to Karen. The evening talk was mostly about the shooting of Karen and the brigadier. Munroe never mentioned the death of Dolek or Jean Wightman. Once the evening dinner had been cleared away, the brigadier took Ray to one side. Then and only then did Munroe mention the two deaths. Ray told him about the brutal murder of Jean and the poison of Dolek. The only question that the brigadier asked was "the murders related to the death of Professor Churchill" Ray could only answer in what he thought was the truth and that was "yes he believed so". A moment of silence filled the room before Ray asked if anything untoward had happened this afternoon. The brigadier said that they, well Duke heard something out side. Going out though the rear gate, he could not see any one or thing that could have alerted Duke. "Did Duke bound off in any particular direction "ask Ray? Startled by the question the brigadier looked at Ray. The brigadier mentioned to Ray to follow him to the rear gate. Stepping out into the dark night the rain falling causing a slight mist. The only light was that of the moon casing a warm glow over the open field. The brigadier pointed to the far distance tree line on the left of the clearing. Ray could see the post parker he had left earlier. The brigadier turned to look at Ray tapping him on the shoulder, Ray turned to face his father. "What going on"? Asked the brigadier. Both men walked back inside the warmth of the manor, before Munroe answered. He told him of the lone tyre tracks hidden under falling branches. The foot prints leading to the clearing the same direction that Duke had gone. The brigadier was shocked in the thought that his home had been spied upon. Walking further into the manor the brigadier stopped again, turned then walked back to the rear door. Ray watched him, he saw his father turn the handle making saw it was firmly locked. Satisfied it was locked he re-joined Ray with a smile on his face.

Both men re-joined the rest of the family. Ray walked over to where Karen was sitting. Close to the fire, Karen looked tried and pale, Ray gently helped Karen to stand. Elizabeth followed behind stopped at the door and tenderly kissed Karen good night. Ray placed his arm around Karen's slender waist slowly they both climbed the staircase. Entering the bedroom Ray moved to the window closing the curtains. Karen started to get ready for bed. Ray walked over to her laying her nightdress on the bed. Once in bed Ray sat beside her, he asked if she was ready to talk about the shooting. Karen nodded. Karen talked for a while, Ray listening all the time. Once she had finished Karen closed her eyes remembering the shooting and the look of the stranger with those piercing eyes. Munroe asked only one question. Karen opened her eyes looking stunned in the way that her husband had asked the question, Karen replayed in a one-word answer “yes”.

Both sat in quietness before Karen broke the silence asking what Rays day had been like.

He began by telling Karen that both Jean Wightman and Dole where dead. “How” asked Karen.

Ray walked over to the chair near the window. Carrying it back to Karen, he told her that Jean had been shot at close range and Jean had poisoned Dolek. Even before Karen could open her mouth, Ray continued with the hour-by-hour account of the day’s events.

When he had finally finished Munroe walked over to the window, trying to place the final piece of the puzzle together. The last part of the puzzle would take both the Munroe’s on a race that would end in blood.

Karen asked Ray if there was any connection between the murder of the professor Churchill and those of Dolek and Wightman. Ray turned away from the window to face Karen when he did speak his words were alarming. He told her that the deaths of all three were in some way connected. They all had a common link with the missing plains. The two new deaths had in some ways a hand in the torcher and brutal killing of the professor. “How” asked Karen.

When the professor had first come to Lincoln, he was followed, by Kessler this we know. Who handed over the task to Hans Smut? Kessler had posted him information and photos so Hans new who to look out for long, before he stepped foot at St Marks station. "How did Kessler know all this?" Karen asked. Munroe was quite for a while before he continued. Remember what Dalton had told us in London that this was all a game to catch Kessler, what he forgot to mention was that this so called game was just a front in finding out the real spy. Kessler was the black pawn on a chessboard the real spy has yet to be caught. Kessler was taken orders from Berlin passing his information on to-let's call him Mr X said Ray. A person who knew him - the professor, planned this. He even knew that Churchill had been employed by the air ministry to engage in the developing of a new tracking system. What he did not know was how and where the development would take place. He figured it out it had to be here in Lincoln, the home of the Royal Air Force. Hans was told to enlist with the help of Kessler two keen people. Hans first victim to black mail was Dolek. Who happened to live next door to the Watson, the boarding house where Churchill would be saying? "How did he know where Churchill would be saying?" asked Karen. Mr X new this along with the train he would be catching. All the information relating to the professor travel and boarding house was known by a select few so it was easy to get everyone in place long before Churchill arrived. "But still with this information we are still missing the key point" said Karen. Ray looked puzzled by what Karen had just said. "Witch is" asked Ray. Karen recalled the meeting they had in London going back through the conversation. Her eyes opened wider when she realised the informant must have come that office, it is the only possible link, which links all this together. The location of where Churchill would be saying even down to the time the train left London it must have come from that office. Munroe considered what Karen had said. It made sense but proving it would be hard. Karen placed her arm on Rays then said "what about the butler Mr Lowe" According to Mary; Mr Lowe had gone to Scotland. I have asked John-Smith to make a phone call to see if Mr Lowe is their said Ray. Munroe was quite for a long time before Carrying on with the story. Munroe told Karen that Dolek was polish who came over to England in the mid-twenties after the First World War with his parents and sister. Hans along with Kessler had done their homework in finding out that Dolek father was working for the Polish government as a spy, against the new German government being set up by Hitler. The Polish new that a pending invasion might happen at any time, his job was to find out when. Unfortunately, for him he was eventually captured entering back into Germany before he could find this information. "How do you know all this" Ray told Karan that Dolek had told him this before he was arrested. "Did he know Hans by name?" No all this was told by another person who Dolek had only met once before. John-Smith found out by chance. Kessler had told Dolek about his father. He black mailed him in thinking that if he helped him he would be saving his father; Dolek did not have a choice. “What was Dolek task in all of this?” asked Karen. Munroe said he had to make note of the time he went to work and what time he came home, this lasted for a few weeks. A pattern was forming with an opportunity to carry out the task witch Smut was assigned. The only fall back was the Wilson; Smut had to get them out. As it was by the time the players were in position Christmas was fast approaching witch made the planning easier. The window of opportunity was three days’ plenty of time to abduct Professor Churchill torcher him found out were the blue print were then just vanished. “What went wrong?” asked Karen. Churchill was the problem. He was stronger than, any of them could have realised. The torcher he endured was something you would only read in a book; still he did not break his silence. Finally, they had no option but to kill him. “So why come after us?” Munroe answer surprised Karen. They knew that his death would be investigated by the local police, all they had to do was wait and watch the players that were involved-us. Nevertheless, why try to harm us; surly they would what us to find the blue print first. Munroe took his time in the next reply. Before he could answer Karen closed her eyes she was feeling tried she had a lot to take in. Munroe gently moved the bed cover to keep Karen warm. He bent over and kissed Karen’s forehead. Before turning, the light out Munroe retrieved a spare blanket wrapped it around himself and settled down in the armchair near the fire. Both the Munroe's were soon fast asleep.

26

Munroe woke with the rap tap on the bedroom door. Pulling the blanket from his aching body Ray eased himself to the door. Outside the faithful butler, John Knight informed him that John-Smith had called he was wonted down at the station. Munroe thanked him. Ray quickly changed. Before he left, he wrote Karen a note placing it on her bedside cabinet. Less than an hour Ray Munroe was at the police station.

Karen feeling better looked around the room. She noticed the blanket spoiled on the floor. Her eye then caught the note Ray had left informing her that he had been called to the station and would see her later. Finishing of the note with love and kisses. Karen gently placed her feet on the warm carpet, standing up right and feeling better, she walked the short distance to the bathroom. Slowly Karen turned the bath taps on watching the steam rise from the filling bath. Once the bath was full, Karen slipped out of her nightdress dipping her tow into the steaming clear warm water. It felt good easing her aching shoulder. Karen placed her head on the end of the bath letting the water work its magic.

Karen sensed that she had company quickly opening her eyes to see Mary Churchill standing over her watching. Mary smiled telling Karen that she had heard the bath water running and came in to see if she was all right. Mary had noticed Munroe leave and knew that Karen was on her own.

Karen had never shown her naked body to another woman before, the only person to see her like this was Ray. However, Karen felt at ease with this situation. She noticed that Mary was wearing her night attire. The outline of her frim breasts was clearly visible. Karen moved her eyes down to her pubic black hair. Karen thought that she had a wonderful body. The stare was broken when Mary asked if she could help her. Karen told her, her bathroom towel was hanging over the chair in front of the fire. Mary turned around at the same time her nightdress came open with her movement. Karen told her that it was all right, as she was naked any way. Mary laughed and slowly walked out from the bathroom to fetch the towel. Karen eased herself up from the depth of the bath. Standing with arms, folded Karen waited for Mary to return. Holding the towel open Mary walked forward to place the warm towel around Karen shoulders. Stepping out from the bath with the help from Mary. Karen placed her left foot on the warm carpet, lifting her right leg Karen accidently brought a cascade of water splashing over Mary soaking her nightdress. Both laughed, Karen let the towel slip from her shoulders if fell back wards into the foaming water. With the help from Mary, Karen walked into the bedroom. The warmth from the glowing fire soon dried Karen's naked body. Karen looked at Mary standing beside her, her nightdress dripping small partials of water on to the reach coloured carpet. "Take your nightdress off "Karen said. Mary hesitated before slipping the cream embodied nightdress from her slender body. Karen watched as Mary slowly pulled the garment over her head. She noticed her breasts rise with the movement of her arms, her nipples porting in a sexual jester. Mary started to shiver, Karen turned to face her. Slowly placing her arms around Marys body bring her close too hers. Mary feeling the sexual pleasure wrapped her arms around Karen. Both naked bodies could feel each other. Karen looked down realising their nipples were touching. Karen brought her eyes to meet Mary's both new what would come next. Slowly they both brought their mouths closer to each other. Their lips parted exploring each other's mouth. Karen ran her arm down Marys back over her frim buttocks moving round to her inner thigh feeling Mary's pubic hair. Mary moved her legs apart letting Karen's hand slide between her legs. Karen could feel the wetness of Mary. Mary sensing her pleasure did the same to Karen. Karen already had her legs open waiting for Mary to touch her. Both could sense that each other was about to climax. Both increased the movement of hands and figures before the final explosion of passion. Still locked together each smiled. Mary let go of Karen naked body and walked towards the bedroom window, pulling the curtains apart. Karen watched Mary's slender body her frim buttocks moving from side to side. Mary turned around her out stretched hand bickering Karen over to join her. Karen hesitated before making the short distance to Mary. Both stood gazing out at the morning sun breaking thought the tall trees. Mary clasped Karen's hand in hers quizzing it tightly. Both stood in silence. Karen was the first to speak when she did it was calm and quiet. "I have never done that with a woman before". Mary turned her head to look into Karen's eyes smiled then said, "Neither have I" Just then a knock on the door announced that breakfast was ready.

Mary gave Karen a passionate kiss before walking to the door. Karen stopped her before Mary had chance to turn the handle. Looking puzzled Mary turned around and noticed that Karen was holding her nightie. Karen helped Mary slip it over her head touching her nipples as she did, the pleasure she felt in the touch excited her more. When the door was closed Karen leaned her back against the wood frame her hands clasped be hide her. Her thoughts darting back to those few minutes together.

27

Ray Munroe entered the police station just before 8.30am. John-Smith was waiting in the office. "What so important" remarked Munroe entering the room. John-Smith met him half way and handed the police report from Scotland. Unfolding the report Munroe studded the in-depth findings from Scotland. Along with the report was a photo of a man fishing, holding the casing fishing line in his right hand. Making him left-handed. Looking closely Munroe could see that it was Mary's butler. John-Smith broke the silence by saying that Mary was telling the truth about Mr Lowe. Munroe slapped the report down on the table he was certain that the man they were after was he. Just then, the duty sergeant came through the door informing both detectives that the police surgeon wonted to see them straight away.

Munroe pulled up outside the mortuary. The sun was just breaking through the clouds when they entered the building. It felt cold and lifeless even though people where moving about. The door the detectives headed for had one signal word embody on the clear window was autopsy. Munroe knocked then walked in. The first sight that they came across was the stainless steel table. Laid upon it was Jean Isabella Wightman. Her chest lay opened to reveal her internal organs. John-Smith noticed a small stainless still dish with both Jeans kidneys and liver laid with in them, blood still dripping from where surgeon knife had made the incision. John-Smith had a closer look all body parts looked like charcoal cooked to a very well done dish.

The surgeon walked to his desk when he heard the detectives enter the room. "Gentleman thank you for coming" Munroe moved his eyes from the sight of Jean to Doctor Leeming. "I have done the post-mortem-as you can see. The report findings along with the bullet wounds are all in here, indicating to the report. "So why ask us down here," enquired Munroe. Doctor Leeming took a moment before moving to the stainless dish. First, if the bullets had not killed her then the cancer would have. She had a matter of weeks at the most to live. She must have been in that much pain. I found traces of morphine in tablet format still inside her digestive system lots of them. Munroe understood now what hold they had over her. If the hospital had found out, she would have been finished.

Munroe looked at Doctor Leeming something else was on his mind, when he did speak Munroe realised that this was the reason why he wanted. Doctor Leeming continued by saying that they had found a small amount of residue under her right index finger. The repot has only come back said Leeming. The Report indicates a formula used in suicide the same found in Dolek's body. The report all so indicates that it was not produced here in England. "How can you be so saw?" asked John-Smith. This formula has a unique element to it. The normal suicide capsule takes a matter of seconds once it enters the body system before the person is dead. This new formula can take up to 30 minutes. The formula is broken down into a watery substance. In a way it can be smeared on any item were the target is going to drink or eat from. As this formula is odious and colourless no one would be any the wiser until it was too late. John-Smith wonted to know how Doctor Leeming could be hundred percent curtain that this formal was not made in England. Leeming turned to his table moved a few papers finally finding the one he was looking for. Turned around and handed it to John-Smith. The bottom line signature read Professor Schrodek. Before John-Smith could answer the next question, Dr Leeming explained.

Professor Schrodek and I shared the same room at Oxford. We were both studying medicine in the early twenty. He was always experimenting with different types of medicine trying to find a formal that would help patents die in a humane way. What he discovered is what we see today. Munroe spoke aloud what he said was to the point "you mean kill". Doctor Leeming looked across at Munroe standing over Jeans body; he knew what he had said was true. John-Smith interrupted the quietness of the room by asking if this professor was still in this country. Dr Leeming answered that as far as he knew he was now leaving in Berlin. He heard that he Schrodek had joined the party that this Hitler had started up.

Munroe had one final question. "Did this Schrodek ever have this formal developed" Leeming clasped his hand around his spectacles before he answered. Professor Schrodek paper was only revelled to me. All his research was carried out behind closed doors. As far as he was concerned as soon as he was happy with his result then that was the last time he ever mentioned it. He knew that he had no chance in ever getting it passed through the medical board. He had developed a formal for killing people, but in his mind, he was helping people who were already dying a slow and painful death. John-smith wonted to know why he had the paper. Leeming told them it was sent it through the post. "When" asked Munroe. Leeming checked the postmark on the envelope, three days ago, from Berlin. Why would he send his findings after all these years asked John-Smith? Munroe stood still and quite for a while, then suddenly turned around. What he said next made both other men in the room gasp. "He sent it to help us find the killer" "How" Leeming said. The professor new that developing this he would be responsible for the death of hundreds or even thousands of innocent people. It is his way of making amends, and in a way telling us that the killer is German. "But how did he know that this killer would be using this" asked Dr Leeming. Munroe did not have an answer to that question. All he knew for curtain was that the killer would go to any lengths in getting his hands on the blueprint. All we have to do now is find him.

Both detectives started to leave the room. Munroe was the last. He stopped and without looking back asked the Doctor when Jeans body would be ready for her parents to collect. Doctor Leeming informed him her body would be ready for tomorrow.

Outside in the car park both detectives let up a cigarette taking in deep breaths before letting out the smoke to drift away. "Where now" asked John-Smith. It is about time we saw the Wightman's said Munroe.

28

Wolf Zimmerman waited on the empty street corner. Checking his watch, he noticed that Hans Smut was late. Just then, the distance headlights of a lone car approached him. Pulling to a stop alongside Zimmerman, Hans could see that he was not happy. Once inside the warmth of the car Zimmerman turned to look at Hans his face expression said it all. Hans uttered the word sorry. Zimmerman nodded then told Hans to drive. Soon Zimmerman found what he was looking for and told Hans to pull over. Once outside Zimmerman walked the sort distance to the red phone box. Inside he dialled a series of numbers and waited. Hans looked across at the man in the phone box, he depraved him to point he could easily kill him for what he had asked Jean to do. His memory darted back to the last time he saw her, how he missed her. Hans told himself once this was all over he would ask her forgiveness. Little did Hans know that Jean Wightman's bullet riddle body lay naked on the mortuary table exposed for all to see?

Zimmerman walked back with a smile fixed to his brutal face. Hans looked at him without saying a word. Wolf Zimmerman rubs his hands together "things are going to plain," he said. "What do you mean?" asked Hans. The call I just made confirmed that the police are looking in the wrong location. Me assonate said that the police had called to confirm I was, were I was supposed to be. Hans looking puzzled by this he wanted to ask but decided not to. Instead, he asked Zimmerman where he wanted to go. “It is about time we made our self’s known to the ladies of the manor” Hans turned the car around and headed though Lincoln up Bunkers Hill and on towards the manor home of the Munroe’s.

The journey made in silence seemed long but reality was it was a sort drive. Hans was about to turn of the main road, when Zimmerman told him to drive pass the turn of. Half a mile down the road Zimmerman found the dirt track he had noticed on the server map of Lincolnshire. The track was old and bumpy with over hanging branches on both sides. Further, down the widening track Zimmerman found what he was looking for. He told Hans to pull over to the right of the track. Hans slowed down looking to find a descant place to stop. Finally, Zimmerman told Hans to switch the car engine off. Both sat in silence waiting almost hopping that no one would come. This lasted for a while, until Zimmerman opened his door. Standing outside, he viewed the surroundings satisfied he had found the correct place. Bending down towards Hans, Zimmerman told him to open the boot of the car.

Hans had done what Zimmerman had asked for. The boot was full of provisions to last a week or too. Zimmerman led the way followed by Hans. The track hidden by years of overgrowth from the tall trees and grass made an ideal place. Soon Zimmerman along with Hans found the abandon concrete bunker. Built during the last war to act as look out and storage complex the building was abandon once hostilities had stopped. With the aid of a crow bar, the rusty padlock and chain soon fell to the ground. With brutal strength and willpower, the metal-hinged door creaked opened. The damp dark gloomy interior came to life when the touch lights flickered on. In almost a decade, the concrete bunker had laid locked in darkness never seeing light until now.

Zimmerman walked around the square shape building. In the centre of the dust, covered floor laid a sealed cellar. Bending down Zimmerman heaved on the metal handle, only when Zimmerman found it hard to open did Hans give a hand. The cellar door opened to revel a flight of wooden stairs leading down to the storage room. Descending the cracked stairs Zimmerman and Hans stood in utter amazement of the size of the underground construction. To the right pushed to the wall an old writing table. Pen and ink lay were it had been abandon all those years ago. Looking further down the narrow side of the cellar were rows of shelves all empty. At the far end of the underground cellar, Hans noticed a closed door; the key was still inside the lock. Both walked down the dusted covered walkway. Hans being the nearest tried the key, it moved as if it had just been placed with in the lock. The beam of the torchlights darted between the walls. Measuring proximally, twelve feet by ten feet the enclosed room housed four cast iron beds. Two beds Hans noticed where standing up each strapped tightly against the wall. The remaining two covered in dust had bedding neatly placed on them as if their owners would be coming back. Wolf Zimmerman has seen what he wanted to see. He turned to leave the room when Hans grab his arm. His piercing eyes starred at the arm upon his, Hans quickly removed his. Looking down Hans spoke with a hush voice. He wanted to know what would happen next and why they had come here. Zimmerman told Hans that this waving his arms about would be there home for the next week or too. Hans looking puzzled still did not understand the purpose of all this. Wolf told Hans that the time had come to find the blueprint, the only way they could this was to adduct Karen Munroe and Mary Churchill. Moreover, Ray Munroe would hand over what they have been after all this time. “How are we going to adduct two women in broad day light?” asked Hans. Time and patient will be our factor which we have plenty of, said Wolf. Zimmerman told Hans to unload the car. Hans turned around and walked down the narrow dusty corridor to the wooded steps, mumbling to himself as he went.

Once Hans Smut climbed the dust covered wooden steps, did Zimmerman start to remove the cast iron beds leaving the other two securely tightened to the wall.

29

After Mary had gone, Karen lingered against the warm wooden door her eyes closed remembering what had just taken place. Finally, Karen still naked walked to the window gazing at the sight of the sun breaking though the morning clouds. She decided that it would be good to stroll through the tall grass breathing in the pure air of spring. Changed and ready Karen walked down the landing, to the spiral staircase. Entering the dining room Karen noticed that she was the last to arrive for breakfast. The Brigadier stood up when she walked through the door smiling. John Knight the butler pulled the dinning chair out. Once settled John handed Karen a note. It was from Ray informing her that he would be late home; Karen placed it in her trouser pocket. Elisabeth started by asking what their plans were for the day. Before Mary could answer, Karen informed the gathered that she intended to have a long walk. The weather outside was just right for a brisk walk. Mary glanced across the table at Karen smiled then said if it would be all right if she could accompany her. Karen said that she would find it delight full of the company. The children were already playing in the garden with Duke so Mary did not have to worry about them. Once breakfast had ended the woman's excursed them self's. Both walked to wards the main door, stopping to gather their coats on the way. Standing on the main doorstep, Mary turned to Karen. "Which way" asked Mary. Karen lifted her head towards the bright morning sun. "This way" heading in the direction of the long green meadow stretching as far as the eye could see. "Why this way" asked Mary. "The suns warmth will warm our backs laughed Karen. Karen slipped her arm inside Marys for support. Soon they were both out of sight of the manor.

Wolf Zimmerman once finished with the beds followed Hans to the top of the bunker. With the car unloaded, both men started the careful handling of the boxes down the stairs. Hans carried the last of the boxes placing it on the writing table. Zimmerman opened one of the boxes removing a small brown bottle containing chloroform, placing the bottle inside his coat pocket. Hans new what the content of the bottle was used for so did not ask. Wolf placed his binoculars around his neck then started to climb the stairs, Hans followed. Zimmerman without turning around opened the bunker door stepping out into the bright sunlight of the morning. Both men without talking headed off to the clear meadow. Hour later Zimmerman found a suitable place to hide. Bring his binoculars to his eyes Wolf scanned the surrounding area looking for the pray that he was hoping to catch. Zimmerman mission was to obtain the blueprint. How long this would take he was willing to wait and wait whatever the cost. Hans sat down his back against an old oak tree. In the distance meadow, he could see black crows swooping down picking food from a dead rodent. Soon a flock of crows arrived alerted by the concert activity and noise. Hans stared in amazement at the sight of the birds fighting each other for the chance of getting some food. Hans Smut stare was broken by Zimmerman informing him the pray was coming.

Karen and Mary walking, as they had no care in the world were unaware that they had been spotted. They too had noticed the crows swooping down, not far from where they were. Karen looked over her shoulder not realising that they had walked so far. Feeling tiered Karen suggested that they should walk towards the wood line for a rest, before turning back to the manor. Stepping over the small stalls Karen and Mary found the idyllic place. Both looked over the meadow they had just walked over. Karen noticed the wind blowing the tall green grass back and forth, the cooling air swilling around them. Karen rested her head on the falling tree tuck her eyes closed. Mary sat close to her watching Karen sleep. Soon she too felt the need to close her eyes. The past few days had taken the toll on her what Mary needed now was to rest.

Wolf Zimmerman face changed to a smile when he saw both women heading towards them. He quietly nudges Hans bringing his finger to his lips indicating to keep quiet. At the same time pointing in the discretion that Karen and Mary were walking. Wolf kept his eyes on them until he noticed that both had sat down near a falling tree log. Slowly Zimmerman and Smut eased them self-up and started to edge forward.

The distance was near but the quest was far greater. With Zimmerman leading they slowly walked towards the sleeping women. Wolf pulled out the brown bottle from inside his coat pocket turning it upside down to let the liquid soak in to the white cotton pads. Wolf handed one pad to Hans. Hans target was Karen while Wolf targeted Mary. On the signal from Zimmerman both pounced at the same time knocking both women out in less than a minute, it could not have gone smoother if Zimmerman had planned it. Hans looked down at the unconscious women both slumped forward, Hans lifted Karen's right arm letting it flop down. They were both out cold.

With ease, they carried the lifeless bodies of Karen and Mary to the waiting bunker. Inside Zimmerman placed Mary body down on the stone dust covered floor. Lifting the trap door Wolf descended the wooden stairs. Hans still holding Karen started to lower her to the waiting arms of Zimmerman. After a few minutes, Zimmerman returned ready for Mary. Hans waited to close the bunker door. Satisfied he then descended the wooden steps closing the trap door be hide him.

A short distance away from the concealed bunker carried by the warm wind the note that Ray had left Karen finally rested against a fallen branch.

30

Detective Ray Munroe along with John-Smith pulled up to the kerb outside Jeans Wightman home. Ray noticed the front room curtain twitching, a hand holding part of it to one side. Stepping from the car both detectives walked to the main door. Before they had, a chance to knock Mr Wightman was waiting and had opened the door. The hand that pulled opened the curtain had vanished. Mr Wightman showed them both to the front room, his wife sat alone near the window dressed in black. Mr Wightman showed the detectives the empty settee. Munroe noticed the black and white photo of Jean taken in her nurses' uniform proudly displayed above the mantelpiece.

Mrs Wightman asked if they would like a cup of tea. Both said they would. John-Smith followed Mrs Wightman to the kitchen, leaving Ray alone with Fredrick Wightman.

Fredrick not to waste any time asked Ray how his daughter was murdered. Munroe looked deep into the eye of a father torn apart with the death of his daughter. Ray told him the brutal way in which Jean had lost her life at close range after leaving Lincoln prison. "What was she doing there?" asked Fredrick, she was visiting a neighbour of yours Dolek. "Why". The question lingered before Munroe told him. Dolek been arrested in connection with the murder of Professor Churchill. It appears Jean had been, told to visit him by her boyfriend Hans Smut. Fredrick stood up and walked to the window gazing across the street at Dolek's old house. He turned with an expression on his face of not quite understanding of what was, said to him. He shrugged his shoulders in desperation trying to put together what Ray Munroe was saying. He heard Munroe speak about black mail the words travelled to a far distance part of his brain not fully understanding anything. Shacking his mind clear Fredrick finally came back to earth, his first words to Munroe was the word he heard only a few moments ago "Black mail" enquired Wightman. Munroe continued saying that her boyfriend had used Jean. He found out that Jean had been, taken medication from the Hospital. "But why" Munroe hesitated he realised that both her parent had no idea that she was suffering from kidney failure. Munroe asked Fredrick to sit down what he was about to say would be hard for him to understand. Ray told him that when they had visited the post-mortem the surgeon informed him he had found that she had cancer that was inoperable. Wightman sat with his hands covering his eyes. When he finally composed himself, he asked a simple question "How long did she have" Munroe sat in silence before he told Wightman that according to the surgeon Jean had but a few weeks to live. Just then, John-Smith walked in with Mrs Wightman carrying the tea. She gently placed the teapot on the table then sat with her husband. Munroe noticed that she had been crying. Mr Wightman moved closer to his wife. Holding hand's, he looked at her before stating that Jean was dying from cancer. His blunt but to the point remark made Mrs Wightman clasped her weary hands in disbelief in what he was saying to her. Mrs Wightman removed her trembling hands looked across at the detective; their faecal expression confirmed it was true. Munroe waited for the extent of the knowing to sink in.

Ray Munroe wonted to know more about the boyfriend, his next round of questions did not revile anything that he already knew. Both Jean parents had not met Hans Smut. Fredrick had seen them both for a brief period walking, but it was from a distance. He did remember that Smut walked with a slight limp on his left leg. Jean had talked about him briefly only to confirm that he was a part of her life. The conversation during meals consisted on work never her private life.

Mrs Wightman confessed their daughter had never been close, not like other families. She started to cry remembering the past they had spent together, if only our lives had been different.

Munroe stood up it was time to leave. Before the detectives, left Ray informed them that Jeans body was ready for collection. Mr Wightman thanked them as they crossed the doorstep to the waiting car.

John-Smith sat in silence waiting for Ray to start the engine. He looked across at Munroe his hands rested on the steering wheel griping it tightly making his hands turns white. John-smith broke the tension by saying that Mrs Wightman had said that Jean had no right in dying the way she had. Munroe looked across at John-Smith then said, "Then let's find out who did it".

Ray Munroe drove the sort distance to Yarbrough road. This time he parked outside number seven. Ray noticed the curtains of old man Kent pull apart. Munroe raised his arm. John-Smith knocked on the door of number seven no answer. Both detectives walked down the adjoining passageway leading to the rear courtyard. The rear gate was open. Stepping through Ray noticed that the yard and grass area of the house to his surprise was tidy. John-Smith pried though the kitchen window. Nothing out of the ordinary he thought. It looked like he had just finished breakfast; all the pots and plates lay neatly on the draining board. Ray tried the door handle it turned the key was still inside the door. Both looked at each other before entering.

Munroe moved to the sitting room. The fireplace swept, logs stood tall in the wicker basket ready to be, used later. Munroe looked puzzled it all looked so clean and tidy. He moved to the front room again nothing be found to be out of place, it was if he knew he would be getting a visit from yours truly. John-Smith climbed the narrow steps to the bedrooms. He found both beds neatly made. Opening the wardrobe in the main bedroom John-Smith found clothes hanging neatly. He searched the jacket pocket hopping to find something. John-Smith pulled out a torn piece of paper with a date and time underlined in pencil. The date was three weeks ago. Checking under the bed, he found a small suitcase strapped tightly. Heaving the suitcase from under the bed John-Smith lifted it on to the clean blanket. Ray Munroe walked in as John-Smith was about to undo the leather strapping. The brown leather case held three document files. Munroe picked one up he noticed the writing was in German. Inside he found that the handwriting neatly scribes the title Professor Churchill. It was a document on him. As Munroe could not read German, he could understand the meaning of what the files meant. It looked like the file-contained information about the late professor. The other two again full of detailed information one was for Dolek and a name they had not heard of Wolf Zimmerman. Two of the files contained detailed photographs. The one on Zimmerman contained only three hand written pages, no photograph. Munroe placed them back inside the case. John-Smith handed the slip pf paper he found in Smut jacket. Ray looked at it then understood it was the timings of a train, but what train. Munroe holding the case exited the bedroom and made his way down stairs. Entering the kitchen, he placed the case on the clean work surface walked a few paces towards the pantry. Opening the door Ray noticed that the shelves that contained food were empty all but a small wrapped piece of boiled ham. John-Smith looked over Ray's shoulder at the empty shelves talking out loud he said, "He's done a runner". "No" said Munroe if has why take all the food it does not make sense. "So why empty the place" Munroe bushed past John-Smith picking up the case before he turned round and said, "He has gone underground with this Zimmerman chap. How can you be so Shaw? "Think about if you were going to run why take the food. You take the food if you plane to hide," said Munroe. John-Smith took one more look around the pantry and then followed Ray down the passageway. At the end, of the passageway Ray stopped at the neighbour's battered old door. Knocking only once before the old man slowly unlocked the door. Standing with his stained string vest the old man smiled at Ray and invited them in. John-Smith walking into the front room could not help but notice the amount of objects that lettered the floor and chairs. He had never seen such an untidy place. How this old man lived was beyond his understanding? Moving more waste from the chairs, the old man beckons them to sit down. John-Smith had a look at the state of the chair small amount of tiny pieces of food imbedded into the fabric of the chair. The old man before the questions started offered the detectives tea. Both looked at each other before they both said they were fine. Munroe started by asking if he had seen any movement of Smut. The old man moved an old newspaper before seating down. He told them that the last time he had seen Smut was three days ago. "What was he doing?" asked John-Smith. Kent turned his attention towards him and politely said, "He was coming to that". The first day I noticed that he was moving cardboard boxes to his car, box after box I was amazed they all fitted inside his car. After he had finished loading Smut walked back to his house, I could hear a lot of clattering going inside. "How" said Munroe. "How what" said the old man. Munroe readdressed the question-making saw he could understand. "How could you know he was clattering about? "Why I was outside hanging the washing out" John-Smith smiled thinking that the old man was more aware than he let on. "I see," said Munroe. "Did the clattering go on for long? "Oh, about as long as it took me to hang my smalls on the line, I was getting cold so went inside. Then it went silent. The next time I saw him he was carrying a small case towards his car, placing it on the back seat. Smut had a last look at the house noticed I was looking so he raised his arm to wave got into the car and drove away. That was the last time I saw him. "And you say this was about three days ago" Munroe said. The old man rubbed his chin thinking before he finally said, "Yes it must be at least three days," John-Smith noticed down the remarks in his notebook. Looking up John-Smith asked if he could tell us any think more about his neighbour. Only that he was a man who kept himself to himself. Munroe thanked him and said they would keep in touch. The detectives stood up ready to leave. The old man eased himself slowly out of his chair walked the sort distance to the door. The old man stopped suddenly before turning the door handle. He turned around and looked at both detectives with one final question etched on his mind. "What did he do?" asked the old man. Munroe placed his arm on his shoulder he told the old man that he was a suspect in a brutal murder case. He looked sad in the thought that a close neighbour could do something so tradable to another human being. Before they got to the car, the old man had closed the door from the outside world.

Munroe sat looking through the car window as neighbour's came and went. One or two stopped and looked at the parked car. John-Smith lit a cigarette placing the brut matchstick in the already full ashtray. Looking over to Ray, he asked what the next step would be. Munroe still deep in his own world did not answer straight away. Instead, he pulled out the note they had found in Smut bedroom. Waving it in front of John-Smith, he told him they would head down to the train station. Parking outside the station the detectives made their way to the empty platform. Standing to one side Munroe noticed the station attendant talking to the workers, busy finishing of the new building. John-Smith eyes followed the sound of the departing train. He could still make out the red tail lights of the train bound for London.

Munroe walked over to the attendant to draw his attention. Ray reached inside his coat pocket showing his warrant card. The attendant took a step back before he asked how he could help. Ray showed him the slip of paper stating if the date and time had any connection to a train timetable. The attendant reached inside his breast pocket retrieving the timetable of the local trains. One entry was a perfect match. The attendant told the detectives that this date and time was the 9.45 out from London arriving here at 1.45, three days ago. John-smith asked if any one got off the train. He told them he was on duty that day and remembered a very attractive woman and two young children disembarked. An old man and another younger woman were waiting.

When the train stopped, they both made their way down the carriages to meet her. "Anyone else" asked Munroe. The attendant stopped talking for a few minutes. Then he said that a second person disembarked just as the train was about to pull away. "Can you descried him" He was dressed in a long black trench coat with hat pulled down over his eyes. He did stop to look at the new building for quite a while, until I told him that the old one" had been blown up". "What happened the "asked Munroe? He smiled then made his way towards the exit. "Did you see any one waiting for him?" asked John-Smith. 'No, once he rounded the corner he was out of my line of sight'. Munroe thanked him. Both detective walked to the parked car, neither uttered a word, until Munroe said they would make enquiries concerning this Zimmerman bloke.

Both detectives after entering the station noticed DCI Cater waiting for them. Munroe brought him up to date on what they had learnt from Smut home. "What about this Zimmerman" asked Carter? Munroe said he would phone Dalton in London he might have something on him. As both detectives entered the office Munroe's phone started to ring. Picking the receiver up he listed to what the caller was saying. Placing the phone down, John-Smith looked over towards Ray his face had changed to a face of concern. "What's wrong?" "That was the brigadier he said that Karan and Mary had gone for an early morning walk and as yet not returned. John-smith checked his watch noticing that the time said it was 14.40pm. "It's still early and the weather is warm," said John-Smith. Ray smiled knowing that Karan could look after herself. Nevertheless, deep down he sensed that something trebled might have happened to them. Ray picked up the phone and dialled the number for London. Dalton soon picked up; he was surprised to hear from Munroe. Munroe asked if he could find anything out about Zimmerman. Dalton sounding surprised asked where he had gotten the name. Ray explained that they had come across a file found in Hans Smut house. Zimmerman's name been mentioned amongst the files. Dalton told Ray he would make enquires. He then asked Munroe if he thought Zimmerman had a hand in with the murder. Ray paused for brief moment before telling Dalton what he thought. Munroe said that Secondly, Ray told him that there were so many parts of the puzzle missing relating to the professor Churchill death. Dalton voice went quite for a period before he spoke. When he did, Munroe was surprised to hear that Dalton suspected a mole within the office. It was Munroe's turn to go quite. Dalton carried on saying that the mole who he suspected was the Chief Constable sectary. How he was going to prove it would be hard. Therefore, what link does this sectary have with the case? Asked Munroe. Dalton explained that this Zimmerman lives a double life; his alias is unknown. Dalton finished by saying he would call back within the hour. Ray looked across his oblong office towards the clock. He noticed that the time was approaching four 'o`clock.

The echoing sound bounced from wall to wall before Munroe realised his phone was ringing. Placing the receiver to his right ear, he heard the familiarly female voice from the switchboard." Hello Ray" I have a call on line two. Ray thanked her. Munroe thinking it was Dalton was surprised to hear traffic noises coming though the receiver. Finally, the caller started to speak. Zimmerman not wanting to waste any time informed Munroe that he had both his wife and Mrs Churchill. The phone went dead. Ray still holding the receiver to his ear was shocked when John –Smith placed his arm on his shoulder. "What is wrong "Ray turned and looked at his close friend finally the words came out Zimmerman he has Karan and Mary. John-Smith dashed to his desk picked up the phone dialled one for the switchboard. The female voice told him that the caller had phoned from a call box in Wragby. Ray waited until John-Smith has placed the phone. Without asking Joh-Smith told, Ray that Zimmerman had used a call box somewhere in Wragby. Munroe dialled a number for the local police station in Wragby. The duty sergeant answered. Ray quickly briefed him. Before hanging up Munroe told him that Zimmerman was armed and not to be approached.

Ray stood up and walked to the large map of Lincoln. Finding the manor house, near Ryland he placed a circle around it and Wragby. Calculating the distance, he roughly figured it too be about twenty miles. Just then, the phone started to ring. The switchboard told Ray it was the same caller calling from Market Rasen.

Zimmerman told Ray that he wanted the blueprint by the afternoon tomorrow. Otherwise, he could say good-bye to his wife. Half-hour later the switchboard informed Ray that the same caller had just phoned not wanting to speak Zimmerman hung up. Before Munroe had the chance to ask for the location. Ray was informed; the caller had made from the call from Saxby. Munroe walked towards the map circled the other two calls. Standing back, he noticed that Zimmerman was traveling in an anti-clock direction heading back towards Lincoln. While Ray was studding Zimmerman's, where about the phone went for the fourth time, John-Smith picked up. Again, the caller said nothing he was playing a game trying to send the police in all directions. "Where this time" asked Munroe. Rothwell, Ray studied the map it was a quite a distance from the previous location. Munroe circled the village, standing back from the map he was sure that Zimmerman must have a hold up near Lincoln, but where.

31

The duty sergeant stationed at Wragby quickly got the patrol car checking the endless call boxes in and around Wragby. A young police officer already out on patrol had noticed a car traveling at speed through Wragby. Taking down the number plate, he gave chase. Through widening country lanes, he ended up at Market Rasen. The police office pulled up just as the driver was exiting the call box he had seen racing from Wragby. The man stared a moment, appeared to make up his mind, and suddenly sounded more friendly. The driver walked to wards the police office smiling as he did so. “Sorry officer” said the driver. He explained that he did not realise he was driving so fast but said he was in a rush. The police officer did not know what he had stumbled on while looking at Zimmerman. Taking his black notebook out he started to take the details of the car, then turned towards Zimmerman. He noticed that the strangers’ mood had changed from a smiling welcome face to that of a stun face of a person who was contently looking around. Before the officer had a chance to write, his name down Zimmerman pulled out his pistol. At close range, the police officer did not know what hit him. The first bullet knocked him to ground the bullet lodge in his right shoulder. He could feel the warm liquid running down his arm, he felt dizzy from the impact, his mind darting towards his mother asking for help. Zimmerman closed the distance to the fallen police officer. He picked up the bloodstained notebook ripping out the page of his number plate, then placing the notebook on the young police officer. He the officer sensed that his time was soon to end. The last moment of life, he had his mother close with him gently kissing him. The final bullet entered the forehead sending his grey matter spilling on to the footpath a tickle of blood started to Ouse from the exit wound. Zimmerman calmly turned away walked back towards his car and headed off towards Saxby.

Across the country field, an elderly farmer heard the sounding echo of a gun firing. He had known the echoing sound of a rifle fire from the last war, but this sound was different. A sound like a crack of a whip. Placing his pitchfork down the old man hobbled as quickly as he could to where the echoing sound was coming from. Bag, another defying sound. Reaching the cross roads looking towards the phone box he noticed the young police officer. Part of his limp body lay in the road his head resting on the footpath. Blood was running from him to the waiting drain. The framer knelt beside him. A look of sorrow was on his worn face. He had seen his friends blown to pieces in the last war, never imaged that he would see death again. He closed the wide eyes of the young police officer then made the 999 call.

John-Smith picked up the incoming call. A stunned face faced Munroe. Ray stared frighten that the news would about his wife. “What is it?” asked Ray. John-Smith cleared his voice before he told Ray that a police office had been reported shot at Market Rasen. Both detectives hurried out of the office stopping on the way at the police armour. Munroe checked the Smith and Weston revolver before housing it in his shoulder holster. Starting the old Ford Munroe pulled away down Monks Road heading towards the falling officer.

Both approach road ends leading to Market Rasen, were blocked off. Munroe walking side by side with John-Smith was, stopped by the sergeant from Wragby. His face said it all. He told them it was one of his officers and had been in the force for a short time. His mother had been informed the only child. Munroe walked sombrely to the laying corps. He noticed the same horrific wounds he had seen before with Jean Wightman. Turning around standing alone Ray saw the old man who had made the call. Both men stared at each other before Ray walked over. The old man said that he had heard this crack like a whip sound, then came across this. Pointing to the blood stained body. Ray asked if he had seen the vehicle during the shooting. The old man shook his head saying he only heard the distance sound of a vehicle. Ray thanked him then re-joined John-smith. "Any help with the witness" asked John-smith. No but we both know who carried this out. Leaving the scene behind them, they followed the route, Ray hopped, would take them to the killer. Reaching the hamlet of Ryland Ray came a crossroad. To the left would take them back to Lincoln, right would lead to Louth. Turning the wheel, Munroe headed towards Lincoln he was certain Zimmerman was close by.

Munroe put his foot down pushing the old Ford as fast as it would go. He was soon approaching the turn of for the Manor. If he had only slowed down Munroe would have noticed the tier markings on the grass verge leading to the disused bunker. With the scheming of the car tiers, the ford pulled to a stop outside the steps of the grandeur of the manor house. The brigadier waiting on the steps greeted his son and John-smith. Duke bonded towards his master his tail wagging.

Inside the brigadier told them both, what he knew and in which way they had taken, heading to the east pasture. Munroe walked over to the French windows looking at the vast empty space of the pasture. He knew it would take a large force of men to check it. Suddenly Duke sat beside him looking at the same pasture, Munroe looked down at his faithful friend. Smiled then went upstairs to retrieve an item of clothing belonging to Karan. Ray called Duke over, sniffing the item Duke started to bark at the front door. Before they left Ray informed the brigadier what they planned to do and to call DCI Carter.

32

Hans Smut eyed Zimmerman exit the bunker before closing the sealed door behind him. Decending the dusted coated wooden steps Hans made his way down the long earrir corridor towards the sealed intumed door. Hans stopped at the padlocked door, he placed his left ear against the cold metal door listerning for any sound, none was heard. Finding the key he slowly turned the lock open. Stepping in side the dark damp room Hans lit the kerosene lantern both woman had been tried too the up right metal bed frames, in a posture to that of the curivection of christ. Hans noticed the movement of both chests moving lifting there brests high with each intake of breath. He moved infornt of Karen eyeing her up and down. Hans started to un button the damp wet blouse, letting it fall open to expose the frim brest that his eyes were fixed on. Tiny droplets of mosture ran over the exposed nipples. Gravity sending the mosture falling to the concret floor. Hans watched each droplets exploding onto the floor already damp from the lack of air in tumed in a cavity of the unknown. His wide pensive eyes went back to the exposed nipples, suddley he could sence he was being watched. Karen started to wake from the deep sleep whitch had brought them to this place. Her eyes wide in disbelef and uncerten of what lay before her. Karen along with Mary were held captive tied in a way that their was no excape from the tomb cavan of hell.

Karen turned her acking head slowly to the left seeing Mary tied up in the same way. Karen tried to scream no words came from her dry mouth, she relised she had been gagged. Karen looked down at her torymetor who was laughing in the knowledge that he had the power to do anything he wonted to do. Hans eyes fixed on Karens' chest grabed her left nipple between his fingers pinching it tightly. Karens eyes said it all the pain shot though her body at a speed that she had not expeianced before. Karen tired to move her hands free, her body reeling with intense pain. The harder she tried to move the pain just shot though her. Karen's eyes started to weep the salt from sweat making her eyes sting she wonted the pain to end.

On the far wall Mary's eyes slowly started to open to the dusty inclosure. Tied to the metal bed frame Mary looked around her surroundings she noticed Karen at the end of the room. To her horror Mary witnessd the brutal torture Karen was being subjected to. A man standing smiling pinching her left nipple. Mary could tell by the tears rolling down her cheek that she was enduring tenable pain in the hands of this man. By rocking her body Mary tried to distract this madman from the enduring torment he was inflecting on Karen.

Hans turned his head slowly to the right reliseing that Mary had come around. The norise she was making by rocking from side to side on the rustic metal bed frame had stopped Hans inflecting the pain. Final Hans fingures eased the pressure of Karen exposed nipple. The red swelling sight made Karen cry more. Relefe from pain and also sadness she knew that this tormentor would start his pleasure apon Mary. Hans stopped short infront of Mary. Reaching inside his coat pocket Hans pulled out the packet of cigarettes. Standing now infront of Mary Hans blow a colum of smoke in Marys face sending the smoke swiling around her head. Her eyes started to weep from the smoke. Hans did it again and again until nothing was left. By now Marys head was spining round and round dazed and feeling sick from beathing in the smoke. Hans lefted her head up by Marys hair bagging the back of the head hard against the metal springs. When Hans got the response that he wonted he let go of the hand full of hair pulling some of the hair out as his hand slowly made the way down towards Marys chest.

It was the same for Mary. Her blouse being ripped open to expose her. Hans lit a further cigarette blowing at the end to make the tip red hot. Slowly inch by inch Hans moved the glowing hot end nearer and nearer to Marys right nipple. Mary could feel the heat getting closer, her eyes wide in horror in the knowing of what would come. The pain shot though her nipple like she had never felt pain before. Mary moved her body from side to side trying to get away from the pain. It only made her tormentor smile more. Hans eased the glowing end of the cigarette from the nipple his handy work of pain had been inflicted. He turned his gaze to Karen smiled then walked though the door, he would be back.

33

Duke raced ahead bonding over the tall following grass. Both detectives had a hard job in keeping pace with him. Suddenly Duke stopped sensing that her master was too far behind her; he waited until they reached him. Ray patted him on the head letting him know that he was doing a good job. Ray looked around at the open space of green meadow that they had entered. He noticed that to his left was a high raised area leading to the main road. His right the meadow eased off towards the far distance woodland. Duke sat looking left and right his senses told him that Karen had headed of towards the wood. He then started to run as if he knew that his mistress was in danger. Ray and John-Smith followed at a steady jog. Duke sniffed the edge of the woodland trying to find the trail that would lead him to Karen. Duke was still running up and down when the detectives finally caught up with him. Finally, Duke gave a loud bark indicating that he had found the trail. Ray ran towards and knelt down beside him. Both man and animal looked at the depth of the wood. Tiny rays of light creeping though the canopy of the tall trees. Duke walked ahead head down sniffing the ground from left to right. Suddenly not far from the edge of the wood, he stopped at a fallen tree. Ray walked towards it. Stepping over the tree, Ray looked around the seen his eyes caught the sight of a white piece of paper laying trapped between two branches of the fallen tree. Ray bent forward picking up the paper. He noticed it was the note that he left Karan. Unaware to Ray the paper had fallen from Karen`s pocket shortly after she and Mary had been carried over the shoulders of Hans Smut and Wolf Zimmerman. John-Smith came over to Ray looking over his shoulder at the paper. Ray Munroe smiled and handed over the paper. "Where now" asked John-Smith. Ray looked down at Duke he knew that the trail from here on would be hard to follow. "We follow the trodden undergrowth it might give us a clue." Duke led the way.

The trail of trodden ground was easy to follow Ray guessed that Karen and Mary had been drugged and had been carried to where ever. The ground been flattened due to the heavy weight of one person carrying another. John-smith for some reason stopped sniffed the air then called out to Ray. Ray stopped turned around towards his friend. He noticed that John-Smith was acting like Duke sniffing the air. "What are you doing?" asked Ray. "Can't you smell it?" Ray not wanting to be, undone by his friend stood and sniffed the air. Smoke was diffing though the air. Not smoke from a fire but cigarette smoke coming from a dense part of the undergrowth not too far away. Creeping slowly forward they soon came upon a raised part of the ground that was unnatural from the surroundings that they were in. Following the soled maze of the raised shape Ray, stumble on a pipe coming from the ground. Bending down he realised it was an air vent. He could smell the remains of smoke, along with a smell of stale air. John-Smith had carried on out of sight from Ray Munroe. With an almost unnoticeable sound, Ray picked up a whistle coming from a corner of the raised earth. Ray Munroe followed the sound. John-Smith stood in front of a rustic over grown metal door. Both looked at each other. They noticed that part of the undergrowth had been removed making easy entry to the door. Carefully Ray grab hold of the handle prising it open slightly to peer inside. What he witnessed was a dark damp square edge room with tiny slits as windows. He suddenly realised that it was a bunker from the last war. His father mentioned it years ago telling him that it was used for storing military papers. It had been abandon once the war had ended. Ray forgot that this part of history was still here.

Stepping quietly inside both detectives moved to either side of the bunker pistols at the ready. Duke started to scratch the rustic door once he noticed that they had gone inside. John-Smith pulled the heavy door open Duke made straight towards the concealed trap door, pawing the dust and gram away. Ray on his hand and knees started to clear away the debris that coved the door. Surprisingly the trap door opened without any effort. Holding the trap door, open Ray bent his head in side he noticed a glow of light. Suddenly a door opened at the far end he could hear a voice saying he would be back. Quickly and without any Norse Ray closed the trap door. Leistering for any sound both the detectives along with Duke froze. Neither man nor dog made a sound. They could just make out steps walking towards them.

Both listened for the steps to start again. The waiting seemed to take forever until Duke picked the movement of footsteps moving away from them. Ray looked at his watch he gave the echoing sound a good five minutes before the trap door was open again. The time seemed to drag until Ray quickly pulled the trap door open. The open trap door revealed a dark dusty place. It smelt of stale damp air. The humidity made Ray start to sweat after descended the dusty steps first. Once he reached the bottom, he indicated to John-Smith it was safe to follow. Duke waited buy the main door alert and ready to warn his master.

Inside the dark enclosure, both detectives noticed that some of the dusty shelving had rows of boxes placed on them. John-Smith peered inside one open box. It was full of food. The amount of boxes amounted that they could survive for weeks. Ray Munroe slowly edge forward to the distance glow of light coming from under the far door. Munroe slowly pulled the Smith and Western revolver out from his shoulder holster. Looking down he noticed that his hand was shaking. Taking a deep breath, he placed his thumb on the hammer drawing it back until he heard the click. Ray turned and looked at John-smith he smiled giving his friend the reassurance that he wanted.

Ray crept ever closer to the waiting door. He placed his left ear on the cold damp metal door. He could here Smut taking to one of them, no sound came from either Karen or Mary. Munroe could hear Smut telling them he was going to carry on where he had left off. Followed by laughter. Munroe eased away from the door. Stepping further back Ray leaned closer to John-Smith. Whispering as not to draw attention to themselves Munroe told John-Smith that they had to draw Smut out from the locked room; time was running out for Karen and Mary. "We might take him by surprise," offered John-Smith, hopefully.

"And we might end up killing each other in the dark," said Munroe.

John-smith indicated that further back to the trap door was a concealed part of the chamber if they could lure Smut out they might have a chance. Walking along the dust-covered bunker, Munroe suddenly had idea on how they could lure Hans Smut out. John-Smith looked puzzled when Ray walked back to the far end stopping at the steps. Placing his foot on the bottom run, he looked up to the era space above him. As quietly as he could he called Duke to the opening. Duke looked down at his master his tail wagging from side to side. He sensed that his master needed his help, without any command from Ray, Duke started to bark as loud as he could. Munroe turned around and hurried to re-join John-Smith.

The sound of the barking echoed along the full length of the bunker bouncing from wall to wall. Inside the closed room, Smut was standing in front of Karen. A large smile greeted her. He clasped both her breasts in each hand moving them around. Hans could feel himself getting aroused. He suddenly stopped what he was doing then started to undo Karen's trouser buttons one by one. When the last button was undone, Hans slipped his hand inside. He could feel her pubic hair was wet from sweat. Karen squirmed her body from side to side trying hard so Hans would let go of his grasp. Mary looking across at her friend did the same with her own scurried body trying hard to draw his attention towards her. Hans though a glance in her direction smiling leaking his lips as he did so. Hans withdrew his hand took hold of Karen trousers by each side and slowly with pleasure started to pull them down. His wide eyes followed the slow revelling movement of Karen's nakedness as he pulled her trousers down over her slender legs. Karen her eyes full of horror looked across at Mary tears flowing down her cheeks pleading for help. Mary again rattled her metal bed frame trying hard as she could to distract Hans. Mary watched helplessly as Karan's trousers laid furlong on the dusty concert floor. Hans Smut reached behind him retrieving two lengths of new rope. Tying each piece of rope to Karan's ankles, he slowly pulled her legs apart securing the ends of the rope to the metal bedframe. Karen's dignity exposed her far beyond her dreams. She was helpless in stopping Smut doing what he was about to do.

Mary watched the ordeal going on before her. Again, she started to rattle the bedframe trying to make as much noise as she could. desperately trying to help her friend and lover.

34

Wolf Zimmerman viewed the distance framer running to the aide of the lone police officer. Before turning of the main road, Zimmerman stopped his car making sure that his handy work had been successful. He smiled when he noticed that the framer slowly stood up then walked the lonely steps to the red phone box. Zimmerman face showed no emotions to what he had done in fact he was happy in the act of killing. Wolf slowly eased the car forward turning left at the next junction. His mind was else where he knew that Hans was enjoying himself with the women. Before Wolf had departed the dark bunker, he had told Hans that whatever happened while he was away he was to leave Mary Churchill for his own pleasure.

The long twisting road leading to the bunker seemed to take forever. Zimmerman decided to take a different route back. He knew that the police would be soon on the scene of the shooting. Not wanting to attract attention to himself, he kept the speed limit down. Ahead Wolf noticed a lone police car speeding towards him the cars mistakable sound blurring out as it passed. Rounding the final bend Zimmerman pulled over on to the soft verge. The route he had taken took him to the high ground looking directly towards the manor house and the dark secret bunker. Stepping from the car Wolf walked to the forward edge of the hill. With binoculars in hand, he stopped short of the deep slope descending some 100 feet below him. Rising the binoculars to his piecing, red eyes, he slowly adjusted the focus. Wolf

Zimmerman soon picked up the tall chimneystacks of the grandeur of the manor house. Following the contour of the meadow on the far side of the manor Wolf noticed movement leading to the wooded area. Holding the binoculars even tighter, he was shocked to witness that his plane of obtaining the blue print had come to an abrupt end. Heading towards the bunker was a group of police officers carrying rifles. Leading the group of armed police officers was the brigadier. Wolf followed his movement to his horror the brigadier was moving closer to the isolated location of the disused pre-war bunker. Zimmerman followed their progress with deep anger imbedded in his face. Before Wolf final turned away and walked back to the waiting car, he heard the echoing sound of a dog barking. Not long after shots rang out across the sleepy woodland. Zimmerman uttered one word “Munroe” The armed police stood still, the brigadier urging them on with haste. Wolf Zimmerman final view was the brigadier entering the dark sinister bunker. The quest was over.

Zimmerman’s parting words spoken aloud was “we will meet again”.

35

Hans Smut looked over his helpless captive with pleasure. His burning eyes darting all over Karen's body now naked. Karen kept her eyes tightly shut waiting for Hans to enter her. Smut started by liking each bruised swollen nipple in turn. Karen could feel his erection getting harder. Suddenly Hans stopped what he was doing. The feeling of this sick tormented man backing away from her made Karen slowly open her eyes. Karen noticed that Smut was walking towards the sealed door. With relief, Karen along with Mary then heard the distance sound of a dog barking. Karen new that the distance sound was Duke their ordeal would soon be over but at what cost.

Outside the seal door, Munroe along with John-Smith waited. Duke kept up the barking that was getting louder and louder the bouncing echo penetrating both sets of eardrums.

Hans Smut reached for his Lugar pistol laying close to the door. Satisfied that the magazine was fully loaded with 9mm rounds. He slowly pushed the mag firmly into the pistol. With thumb and for finger Hans pulled back on the cocking sild inserting the first round into the chamber. Safety catch was off. Before Hans opened the rustic metal door, he turned around and looked at each of the woman tied and gagged to the bed frames. His eyes darting from one to the other. Karen had the feeling that this would be the last time that they would see Smut alive.

Smut slowly eased the door open. Slowly he inched the metal door wider the sound of Duke barking hit his ears. Hans placed his left hand against his left ear trying to blank out the echoing sound going further inside his head. His eyes fixed on the sunlight beaming down the wooded steps making the dusty surroundings a haze. Before Hans could adjust, his eyes to the hazy glum John-smith stepped out from the concealed part of the bunker. Hans Smut noticed movement not knowing who was there he fired his weapon. Shots rang out flashes could be seen from the barrel of the Lugar. Round after round whizzed pasted Munroe who was still behind the shelving. John-Smith ducked his head after the first round. Rising his pistol to return fire, he was, caught by the 9mm round fried by Hans. The round hit John-Smith in the right shoulder shattering the bone to a plump. The force of the round spun him around. Blood ran in thin streamers down his arm from the gaping wound sending droplets of dark blood on to the dusty floor. John-Smith felt the warm liquid tricking down his right arm. Blood spread though his fingers making John-Smith to drop his pistol. With his back to Hans, John-smith was unaware that Smut had lined up the Lugar's fatal round. Munroe watched his close friend drop to his knees. His face with pain and shock told Munroe that the round had hit vital organs. John-Smith tried to reach the bloodstained pistol laying close by. His fingers slipping to grasp the pistol due to the amount of warm liquid blood. Munroe looked in horror at his trusted friend. Blood started to slip between his twitching lips. John-Smith spat out blood before he could speak. "Kill" the bastard." Munroe moved his gaze towards Smut; he noticed that Hans was changing magazine. Moving away from the concealed location Munroe stood up. Grasping his pistol; in both hands he took aim and fired. The first round sliced of his left ear lobe leaving strands of bloody skin. Smut felt the throb of pain, running though the exposed ear blood now covered his hand. Shock took hold of Hans Smut. Munroe seeing that his emissary was vulnerable fired again. Ray fried again round after round found its mark. Hans's body turned from left to right blood spat from each penetrating wound. The last round fried Ray aimed for the space between Hans Smut piercing eyes. The Smith and Weston bullet travelled though grey matter exerting with a thud. Smut fell backwards with the impact. His body bounced once on the dusty stone flooring. Ray lowered his empty pistol to his side, his hand started to tremble. Looking down Ray noticed smoke coming from the barrel. He followed the trail of blood to the scene were John-Smith was kneeling. Blood dripped from his motional body. Suddenly he heard a distance sound of rattle coming from the closed door. Munroe stepped over Han Smut body, took a deep breath and opened the door. The sight he witnessed shocked him. Tied and gaged to two up turned metal bedframes was his wife and Mary. From the glow of the burning light, he walked over to Karen. Her eyes said it all. Tears where running down her face their ordeal had ended. Quickly Ray untied the rope that had bounded her to the frame. Karen still naked but for her shirt though her arms around him. She held him tight not wanting to let him go. Ray gently moved Karen's arms, bending down he retrieved the trousers laying were Smut had placed them. While Karen slowly got dressed, Ray went over to Mary. Removing the gag that impaled her from shouting for help Mary let out a gasp of joy. Her eyes darted over to Karen watching her pull the trousers over her slender legs. Once Karen had finished she walked over towards her friend. Her legs felt that they could not move with the hours spent tied to the frames. Both women hugged each other. Ray heard movement coming down the corridor. Reloading the Smith and Weston, he told both of them to stand away from the door. Munroe eased the door open. The lone figure walking towards the door carrying a shotgun was the brigadier. Ray walked over to him leaving Karen and Mary inside the concealed room.

"What a bloody mess" said the brigadier? He knelt down in front of John-Smith tears formed in the corner of his eyes. Wiping away the tear, he reached over to the blanket-laying furlong on the shelf left by the some long ago sole. Suddenly the concealed door behind them opened. In the doorway stood Karen and Mary arms around each other. Both starred in disbelief in what had taken place. Pools of red blood covered the floor. Karen eyed the bodies of the dead. She noticed the gaping hole in the back of Hans Smut head. White bone that once covered the brain lay amongst the stained black hair. Karen placed her trembling hand over her month stopping herself from screaming in shock once she noticed that one of the fallen was her friend John-Smith. Ray Munroe with the help from the brigadier helped the woman walk the silent dusty corridor towards the wooden staircase. Helping hands reached down into the glow of the dark bunker. Karen was the last to leave. She suddenly stopped on the second step she wanted one more look at the bunker that had been her imprisonment. Munroe moved towards her placing his hand on hers. With a smile and a nod, Karen climbed the remaining steps to freedom.

36

Out side from the intumed dark bunker in the warm afternoon air Karen along with Mary sat in wounderment of what had gone before them. Karen slowly turned her head when she heard momvment behind her. With tears forming in her eyes Karen wittnessed the lifeless body of John-Smith being carried though the bunker door. Covered in a grey blanket retrived from the deapths of the bunker John-Smith was gentel layed down near a fallen branch shellerted from the late afternoon sun. Ray Munroe walked over towards his wife. His face was taught with angor and sorroy in the death of his friend. Sitting beside Karen, Ray placed his arm around Karen,s shoulders. Tears flooded down her checks, wiping away her eyes Karen looked up at Ray and asked one solitary question. "Why" Before Ray answered DCI Carter came and sat down beside them. He said nothing for a while all three sat in silance waiting for one of them to break the long silance.

DCI Carter hurried to the desused bunker as soon as word had reached him. He knew that questions had to be answerd. From what he was told the answers would come as as shock to all concered. On his arrival he wittnessed the body of DC John-Smith Patten being removed from the bunker, drapped in a blanket. Turning around DCI Carter noticed in a distance clearing hudaled together was the slioate of

the Munroes and Mary. Walking slowly as not to sartel them he made his way towards them. He heard Karen ask the question why. Stepping over the fallen log he sat beside them, all three turned their heads.
DCI Carter looked at earch of them in turn. "You asked why?" Carter said. "Can you tell us then" said Karen not bothering to face him after he had sat down. I can try to place the jigsaw puzzle together.
It all started way before we got the call in investicate the late Proffessor Churchill. I had a call from Scotlanl Yard telling me that they thought a spy from Germany was working in and around Lincoln, his name was unknown but they new about a Captain Fridrick Kessler form the Germany embasstry who was on their watch list. He had been seen on occasion travling past the RAF camps of Waddington and Scrampton plus others. Then I was told that annother player had turned up, again no details was forwarded to me regarding what this person looked like or even a name. It was decided by Scotlandyard and the MI5 to come up with a plain to flush him out.
MI5 new that Germany was interested in our develoment of radar, so they deviced a cuning plane." How did my husband get involded" asked Mary. "That was by a cance incounter. Apparently your husband was having lunch with your cousion Mr Churchill in London. As you know Mr Churchill is well known with in parlyment and it just so happened that he descused this plane with him, why I don't know. Months before he was sent here in Lincoln your husband had numirous meeting with MI5. As you are awear the late proffesor was a man of considable

importance in the field of scieance. His cover story was that he was coming to Lincoln to finalize the protpye for the radar system. The trap was set all that was required now was for the players to arrive. “So went went horrble wrong” asked Karen. Unknown to us all was that the players, well two of them was already here. MI5 in London concentrated on Kessler to make his move unawear that Proffessor Churchill had already been captured, hence the request to find him by witch time it was to late. “Why? Didn’t the proffessor just had over the flause files” said Mary. He was trying to give us time so we could arrest the fugetives, but in the end what they did was to much for him to bear. “And Wolf what was his part in it all” asked Munroe. DCI Carter said that as far as they could work out Wolf was a go- between relying information to Kessler. What we did not relise at the time was this other person Zimmerman showing up. No one new who he was or where he is now he has just vanished. As you know Kessler was shot down over the english cannel with the surposed documents. The real radar system was invented by Robert Watson-Watt at Bawdsey Manor Felixstowe 1st September 1936 and is operational as we speak. Munroe looked stright ahead before asking the next question. He already new the answer before Carter comfried it. “What about Jean Wightman” asked Munroe. Carter cleared his thorght before speaking. Jean Wightman had an afear with Wolf. He, Wolf new that once the proffessor had lodge with the Wilson,s she would meet him-whitch she did. He on the occassions that they met would ask about the proffessor. Wolf was gathering information on the day to day activaty of the proffessor at the same time giving Jean morphine for her condition. He used her her in every senice of the word. She had a passion for sex witch he was happy to perform. "Did Wolf kill her" asked Karen. Carter turned his head to look at Karen. No said Carter he Wolf didn,t known that she had been killed. We think it was Zimmerman who did all the killings even the death and torure of the proffessor. "What hold did he have over Wolf" asked Mary. Carter stood up from the fallen log stretching his legs as he did so. Before he aswered he reached inside his coat pocket for a park drive. Lighting it up he took a long drag inhaleing as he did so, blowing the smoke high to the canopy of trees before Carter lowered the cigarette. We now know that Kessler and Zimmerman worked together during the Spanish civil war between 17July 1936 to 01 April 1939 inflecting pain and torure to the young and old. As for Hans Wolf all we can gather from the files is that his parents are jews leaving in Berlin. This may or not have any bearing on why Zimmerman enrolled him into working for him. We shall never know the answer. All three sat for a long time once DCI Carter had finished.

Munroe caught the movement of the ambulance arriving stopping a distance away from the bunker. Ray looked at Karen and Mary saying that it was time to go. Both women surpoted by each other gingerly stood up to walk the distance to the waiting ambulance. Munroe held Karens hand tigthly he had lost her once he did not want to losse her again.

Wrapped in the same blankets both women sat huddled together. Ray wisped into Karens right ear before the doors were closed. Standing at the rear of the ambulance Ray Munroe watched as the ambulance made its slow drive to the main road. Turning around Munroe noticed that Wolfs body was being carried to the second vechile by two policeman. Suddley the rear policeman stumble over a fallen branch tillting the strecher to one side. Wolfs left arm flooped out side the blanket blood dipping onto the reach green grass. What caught Munroe eye was the sudden falling of an objet not noticed by the policeman. Slowly Munroe walked over picking up a gold ring coverd in blood. Whipping the ring clean Ray looked inside and read the words "Always my Love" further on around the inside was a date 1924. Placing the ring into his pocket Munroe watched as the doors closed on the ambulance taken Hans Wolf away.

37

Karen spent a week in the county hospital along with Mary. Their friendship growed by each passing day. Mary told Karen that she would take the children back to London. Her work was there and it made sence for that work to be completed. Karen told her that she was more than welcome to come down to the manor any time she and the children wanted, the door was always open.

Finally Munroe got the call saying that his wife was ready to go home. Making sure the house was clean and tidy Ray along with Duke made the steady drive towards the hospital. He had been told that Karen would be waiting in the folower garden within the court yard of the hospial. Duke laid down infron of the Ford car watching Ray head of towards the main entrance. Following the signs Ray soon found the court yard. Karen was sitting in the bright sunshine with her back towards the door. Ray stopped at the door gazing though the window watching Karen. He noticed that she had picked up a brocken stem of a rose and holding it close to her noise to inhale the sweet smell. She had gone though an ordeal of which he didn,t want to see again.

The court yard door opend with slight hiss, Karen turned her head around noticing that Ray was walking towards her. Karen stood up and with that she ran into his opem arms kissing him. Ray held her close. He could feal Karens body tremble with emotion. Finally with hands locked together they made there way outside. Duke noticed them exit the main entrance not waiting to be called he bounded over as fast as his legs would go. Karen bent down to give him a hug. All three with Duke in the middel walked back to the waiting car.

Days passed by for the Munroes after Karen had come out of hospial. September 1939 brought endless sunshine. The local wireless sation brourgth up to date reports on the prime Minister Nevell Chambelin visit to see the cancollor of Germany Herr Hitler. The hole of the counrty was on tender hooks waiting for his return. On the 3rd of September 1939 the prime minister of England announced to the nation that a sate of war had been decleared betwwen Great Britain and Germany.

Sitting together with Duke, Ray and Karen Munroe listed to that announcement boradcasted to the nation that war had been decleared. Both looked at each other, just then the phone rang……

To be continued

OTHER BOOKS BY THE AUTHOR

With Britain on the verge of war Detective Sergeant Ray Munroe finds himself pitted against a nemesis that will do anything to get his hands on a certain blueprint, even kill in cold blood. The race is on before war is declared

Set in the idyllic countryside of Lincolnshire. The story is gripped with suspense, thrills, twists, and turns. The deadly cat and-mouse game has just begun.

CPSIA information can be obtained at www.ICGtesting.com
Printed in the USA
BVOW01s0208160816

459031BV00028B/100/P

9 781534 757707